THE QUEST FOR MEANING

Open Your Eyes in the Pursuit of Purpose

Kamal Mistri

Published in the United States of America

Published by Mercury Publishing LLC

First Printing Edition, 2024

PREFACE

Are you adrift — floating through the vast expanse of the world without any rhyme or reason? It sure can feel like it at times. The truth, for many of us, finding our purpose can be elusive. What even *is* a purpose other than an overused trope that has been peddled to us in popular culture? Why have we been made to feel as though if we don't find this elusive thing, we are not whole human beings? Are we subpar or less than simply because we don't have some profound hero's journey behind us or ahead of us? And who came up with that word, anyway?

Well, I — at the very least — have an answer to the latter: Aristotle.

But that's neither here nor there.

The main question here is: are you adrift?

If you are, I want you to know that many of us grapple with questions about our purpose and what gives our existence true meaning. Beyond the endless chase for success and material wealth lies a longing for spiritual fulfillment that nurtures our souls and connects us to something greater than ourselves. For countless people who have dreamt of fame only to be left feeling emptier than before, they failed to realize that it wasn't fame on their mind. It was the desire to capture the hearts of many. And at the root of the desire to capture the hearts of many was the longing to make a difference in the lives of all of those people.

There is always an underlying meaning to the desires that we ***think*** will fulfill us.

The point is that it's easy to feel adrift — disconnected from our true selves and the world around us. We crave meaningful connections and experiences that transcend the superficial. We wish to experience things that have the ability to touch the core of our being. This is where our spiritual journey begins. It is a path that invites us to explore the depths of our soul and discover what is truly important to us.

Consider this the beginning of your journey into self-discovery and personal transformation. It's about finding your spiritual essence and bringing it to the forefront of your everyday life. It's about understanding that every moment, every choice, and every experience contributes to your spiritual existence and, thus, your sense of purpose. But take note of the fact that I said a ***sense of purpose*** and not just ***purpose***. That is because (spoiler alert) you already have a purpose simply because you exist.

The point of this book is to find meaning through spirituality. And spirituality is more than just a personal endeavor. It's a living, breathing presence that permeates our interactions with the world. Every act of mindfulness, every moment of gratitude, and every instance of compassion has the power to enrich our spiritual journey. Through our commitment to personal growth and our willingness to connect with the divine — whatever form that may take — we can create a life of fulfillment.

Why Did I Write This Book?

Preface

I wrote this book to help those who have felt the pangs of purposelessness in a world often obsessed with the material. Deep down, we all have the desire to understand our purpose and connect with something greater than ourselves. In an age where material success is frequently equated with happiness, many of us find ourselves feeling empty and spiritually adrift.

My goal with this book in *The Pursuit of You* series is to explore the importance of spirituality in all its forms — from personal introspection to the universal search for a higher purpose. This, I believe, is important because our spiritual journeys shape our experiences and influence our well-being in a number of ways.

Ultimately, this book is about rediscovering the joy and fulfillment that come from embracing our spiritual essence. It's about finding meaning beyond your worldly pursuits and creating a life that feels interconnected enough to enjoy those pursuits in the event that they actually pan out. By understanding the importance of our spiritual journey and learning how to nurture it in our lives, we can create a more enlightened and fulfilled world for ourselves and others.

As with all of my books, it is trust and a strong sense of resilience, as well as a love for others, that propelled me to write this book in order for "YOU" to appreciate the beauty of this life journey which only "YOU" can make a sanctuary for your wellness, well-being, and happiness.

So, I invite you to go on this quest for meaning with me.

Preface

Table of Contents

The Quest for Meaning: Open Your Eyes in the Pursuit of Purpose

Part I: The Foundation of Meaning

Part II: Getting to the Core

Part III: Practical Paths for the Present

Table of Contents

Part IV: The Road Ahead

KAMAL MISTRI

The Quest for Meaning: Open Your Eyes in the Pursuit of Purpose

Part I: The Foundation of Meaning

CHAPTER 1 –

THE DOORS TO SELF-DISCOVERY

The discovery of the self requires an honest and introspective look into your inner workings. What is it that makes you tick? How do you view the world? How do you relate to those around you?

The reason why self-discovery is a crucial part of spirituality is that it allows you to see the truth of the matters that are all around you. It allows you to examine what is most important to you and where your values truly lie. In so doing, you not only give yourself the permission to step into the most authentic version of yourself, but you also begin attracting the right energies into your sphere of existence.

Ultimately, being able to understand yourself and have an awareness of who you are will become one of your greatest strengths. It will set you up for spiritual success as well as material and emotional success. In the long run, this is an incredibly freeing step. After all, people can only poke holes in tarps that are meant to block out pieces of you from view. When you bring all of those pieces to light, there will no longer be a proverbial tarp for people to poke holes in.

That said, before we dive into the actual journey, it's a must that we understand it fully.

Understanding the Path

The beginning of the road to self-discovery is often marked by discomfort and uncertainty. As you get started, you can expect to experience a range of challenging emotions and situations. Initially, there may be a sense of disorientation as you begin questioning familiar patterns and beliefs. This can lead to feelings of confusion and doubt as your previous understanding of your "self" and life starts to unravel.

This is perfectly normal, so don't be discouraged. Instead, try to see this time of upheaval as an opportunity for immense growth. Nonetheless, knowing what some of the signs and symptoms of this period might be can help put you at ease. After all, human beings are inherently drawn to what we know as opposed to that which we don't. With that in mind, one of the first experiences on this path is the confrontation with inner turmoil. Long-buried emotions such as **fear, anger, sadness**, and **anxiety** often surface. These emotions can be overwhelming and may cause you significant discomfort. You may feel as if you are losing control or facing an identity crisis. Remember that this emotional upheaval is a natural part of the process as it signals the beginning of deep inner work.

That level of discomfort will also arise from facing aspects of yourself that have been suppressed or ignored. This includes acknowledging your flaws, past mistakes, and certain aspects of your personality that you may feel are less than flattering. This is precisely why the initial phase of self-discovery requires an honest self-assessment, which can be painful. It involves looking at yourself without your usual defenses and confronting uncomfortable truths. Spiritually, the beginning of this journey often involves a sense of existential uncertainty. Long-held beliefs and assumptions about life as well as your purpose and the universe may come into question. This can lead to a feeling of being adrift as you grapple with finding new meaning and understanding. The spiritual aspect of self-discovery may involve seeking answers to deep questions, which can feel unsettling and isolating. This is especially true if that questioning act leads you away from long-held beliefs that might connect you to those around you. But we'll discuss this in a later chapter.

What's important to note at this point is that there is also a physical aspect to this discomfort. As emotions and spiritual insights arise, they can manifest in physical symptoms such as **fatigue, restlessness**, or even **physical pain**. This is known as a "somatic response" and it is a reflection of the deep changes occurring within. As your body processes and releases stored emotions and tensions, you will run into these physical manifestations.

Needless to say, you can expect to encounter resistance on both an internal and external front. Internally, your mind may resist change and cling to familiar but limiting patterns and beliefs. This resistance can manifest as procrastination, self-sabotage, or a strong desire to revert to your old ways. Externally, you might face skepticism or opposition from others who are accustomed to your previous ways of being. This external pressure can add to the sense of discomfort and challenge that you experience. Sadly, this is where most people draw the line and give up. Try not to let this happen. If you can overcome the initial stages of discomfort and grief (yes, grief is a part of this too), you will thank yourself for it further down the line.

Grief for the old you and your old life tends to creep in due to the significant amount of solitude and introspection that you go through at this stage. This can lead to feelings of loneliness as you distance yourself from external distractions and superficial interactions. Spending time alone with your thoughts can be daunting, but it is essential for gaining deeper insights and understanding. Just know that amidst the discomfort, you will experience moments of clarity and great insight. These moments will provide you with glimpses of your true self and offer encouragement to continue the journey. However, they are often fleeting in the beginning and overshadowed by the prevailing sense of uncertainty.

Ultimately, the beginning of the road to self-discovery is about breaking down old structures and making way for new growth. As you can imagine, this was never meant to be an easy stage. The treasure at the end of the tunnel is not something that this version of yourself can grasp.

You must shed this weight before you can take hold of the reward.

Becoming Self-Aware

As you begin confronting sides of yourself that were previously hidden, you will take the first steps toward becoming self-aware. This is an incredibly transformative process that involves understanding your thoughts, emotions, and behaviors on a deeper level. You can expect to experience a range of emotions and reactions that span the spectrum of being both enlightening and challenging.

Initially, becoming self-aware can be overwhelming. You might feel a flood of emotions as you start to uncover layers of your psyche that have been hidden or suppressed. This is because you'll be confronting parts of yourself that you may not like or have previously ignored. The process can be likened to peeling an onion — each layer removed reveals another and it often brings tears with it. One of the first things you might notice is an increased sensitivity to your own thoughts and feelings. You begin to recognize patterns in your thinking and behavior that you were previously oblivious to. This heightened awareness can be both empowering and saddening. On the one hand, it offers the opportunity for growth and change. On the other, it can be unsettling to realize how much of your life has been influenced by unconscious drives and habits.

Expect to encounter something known as "cognitive dissonance," which is the mental discomfort experienced when holding two contradictory beliefs or when new information challenges your existing worldview. As you become more self-aware, you might realize that some of your actions and beliefs are not aligned with your core values. This can lead to an internal struggle as you toil over the need to change long-standing behaviors or attitudes. Of course, resistance is a common response during this journey. Facing the truth about yourself can be painful and it is natural to feel reluctant to confront certain aspects of your personality. You might find yourself making excuses, rationalizing behaviors, or avoiding introspection altogether. That's because the more you uncover about yourself, the more you'll remember things that you've done through the lens of this newfound understanding. You'll be tempted to either judge yourself harshly or give up altogether. Try to be gentle with yourself and walk a middle ground here. None of us are given a rule book for life and the mere fact that you are trying to become a better version of yourself is commendable in and of itself.

There may be a tendency to cling to familiar narratives and identities. For example, you might have defined yourself by certain achievements, relationships, or roles in life. Becoming self-aware involves questioning these identities and understanding that they do not fully define who you are. This can be disorienting and lead to a temporary sense of loss or confusion about your place in the world. This then leads to feelings of vulnerability. Acknowledging your flaws, weaknesses, and past mistakes requires a level of honesty that can leave you feeling completely exposed and defenseless. It's crucial to note that this vulnerability, however, is an integral part of the self-discovery process. It is through embracing your vulnerabilities that you can begin to cultivate self-compassion and acceptance.

And just as you're coming to terms with your own understanding of this transition, you'll find yourself dealing with the reactions of others. As you change and grow, those around you might react in unexpected ways. Some may be supportive, while others might feel threatened or uncomfortable with your new self-understanding. This can lead to tension in relationships and further fuel internal conflict as you navigate these dynamics.

Don't give up!

As you become more attuned to your inner world, you'll gain clarity and insight into your motivations and fears. This deeper understanding allows you to make more conscious choices and to live a life that is more aligned with your true self. Moreover, self-awareness promotes emotional intelligence, which enables you to manage your emotions better and to empathize with others. It enhances your ability to communicate effectively and to build healthier, more authentic relationships. Over time, the initial discomfort gives way to a sense of empowerment as you learn to live more authentically.

It is at this point, that you'll need to set your goals.

Setting Your Goals

When we look at setting new goals from a spiritual perspective, we see that it involves aligning your aspirations with principles of inner growth and fulfillment. Unlike conventional goal-setting, which often focuses on external achievements, spiritual goal-setting emphasizes values like compassion, kindness, and personal transformation. To start setting new goals, begin by reflecting on what deeply resonates with your spiritual journey. Consider how your beliefs about life's purpose and your connection to a higher power or inner wisdom can guide your goal-setting process.

To do this, you can get into introspection and journaling to clarify your intentions. These practices create a sense of self-awareness and help you identify areas where spiritual growth is needed. Ask yourself meaningful questions about how you want to contribute to the world and what legacy you wish to leave behind. From there, set intentions that align with your spiritual values rather than solely focusing on specific achievements. For instance, instead of aiming for material success, set an intention to live authentically and contribute positively to the lives of those in a specific locale (perhaps in your home, workspace, or community).

As you define your spiritual goals, seek support from potential mentors, spiritual communities, or trusted friends who share similar values. Discussing your aspirations with others can provide insights and encouragement, which can help you stay committed to your path. Regularly review and adjust your goals as your spiritual journey evolves. Remain open to divine guidance and embrace opportunities for growth. Of course, setting these goals might feel like you're searching for a needle in a haystack if you haven't done the inner work yet, which is why I would like to further assist with that.

*

With a firmer understanding of what it takes to find yourself in the chaos that is life, you will find that the foundations upon which you build your spiritual journey will be equally firm. I can't stress how important that is. When all is said and done, all you have in this life is yourself and your connection to your higher power — whomever or whatever that is for you. When the music dies down and the party is over, it's just you, your thoughts, and the element that drives your inner workings. And so, we can now move on to what might have shaped that side of you: your past.

CHAPTER 2 –

UNDERSTANDING YOUR PAST

Your past is peppered with lessons. There are things that you can look back on with fondness and things that make you recoil. There is pain, heartache, and maybe even betrayal. There are stories that you do not read out loud and those that you wish you could shout from the rooftops.

The point is that your past is a part of you.

And just as your past is a part of you in the present, it is also connected to you in the future. Time, as it were, is non-linear. We revisit certain things because we have not carved the lesson from the rubble of the experience. We revisit people, places, and things in different forms and we re-experience past pains.

That is until we embrace the lesson and move on.

As such, it's important to understand the past. It will give you the ability to see where you might have gone wrong in the past. And when I say "wrong," I'm also referring to the times that you've allowed people to do you wrong continuously despite having seen the signs of their behavior repeatedly.

So, it's not all about being accountable for things you have done to yourself or others but accountable for things you've allowed into your earthly experience.

Reflecting on the Past

Reflecting on experiences that have shaped your current spiritual perspectives is essential for understanding how past events influence your beliefs today. Things such as being spoken down to by religious people, feeling judged, and being encouraged to segregate yourself from those who don't share your family's spiritual beliefs are all negative encounters that could have significantly impacted your spiritual outlook.

Being spoken down to by religious people is something that seems to come up quite a lot on social channels these days and it seems as though this experience can create deep-seated feelings of shame or inadequacy. When individuals in positions of spiritual authority or those who present themselves as deeply religious speak to you in a condescending or dismissive manner, it can erode your sense of self-worth and create a barrier to spiritual exploration. These experiences might lead you to question your own worthiness or the validity of your spiritual journey. In the long run, this can cause you to withdraw or distance yourself from spiritual communities altogether.

Similarly, being judged by others for your beliefs or lack thereof can be incredibly isolating. If you've felt the sting of judgment from those who are supposed to be your spiritual family or community, it can leave scars that affect your ability to engage openly with spirituality. This judgment might have taught you to hide your true self and this may have resulted in you suppressing doubts or questions that you might have had. It can create a fear of judgment that continues to color your spiritual experiences, thus, making you wary of exploring different paths or expressing your true beliefs.

Then there is the pressure to segregate yourself from those who don't share your family's spiritual beliefs. This can be deeply alienating. In your younger years — while in the safety of your familial home — it might feel like these are the ties that bind you together. However, if you've now ventured out into the wide world by yourself and find yourself self-isolating because you judge others who don't align with those beliefs, you might be in for a rude awakening. Ultimately, this segregation can create a sense of division and mistrust towards others, thus reinforcing the idea that your beliefs are superior or that those outside your community are not to be trusted. This mindset can hinder your ability to see the value in different perspectives, which will limit your spiritual growth and understanding. It may have led you to create boundaries that prevent you from forming meaningful connections with people of diverse backgrounds, thereby isolating you from a broader spectrum of spiritual experiences.

These experiences can collectively shape a complex spiritual landscape for you. They may have instilled in you a sense of defensiveness or skepticism towards organized religion or spiritual communities. You might find yourself overcome by feelings of resentment, anger, or confusion about the very concepts of faith and community. Alternatively, these experiences could have sparked a deep desire to seek a more inclusive and compassionate spirituality — one that embraces diversity and encourages open-hearted exploration.

Reflecting on these past experiences is not about dwelling on the pain or resentment but about understanding how they have shaped your spiritual journey. By acknowledging these influences, you can begin to heal and redefine your spiritual path. You can start to question the narratives that have been imposed on you and open yourself to a more authentic and inclusive spirituality. This process of reflection and understanding allows you to reconnect with your true self — a "self" that is free from the judgments and constraints of the past.

Finding Closure for Trauma

Some of these past experiences may have been traumatic at the time or led to trauma in the present. Finding closure for trauma caused by past experiences, especially those involving emotional abuse and narcissism that may not have been recognized at the time, is a deeply personal experience of healing and forgiveness. As you reflect on these experiences, it's important to acknowledge the impact they have had on your emotional and spiritual well-being.

Emotional abuse is often subtle and insidious and can leave lasting scars that affect your self-esteem and relationships as well as your overall sense of worth. It may have manifested in manipulative behaviors, gaslighting, or constant criticism from trusted adults or figures of authority in your life. These experiences can distort your perception of yourself and others, thus prompting you to create barriers to trust and intimacy in future relationships. Recognizing emotional abuse and narcissistic behaviors retrospectively can be enlightening yet painful. It involves coming to terms with the realization that individuals you trusted may have exploited their power or influence over you. This may have caused you considerable emotional harm that has manifested as a resistance to the spiritual aspects that you associated with those abusers. This awareness is a crucial step toward healing as it allows you to validate your own experiences and reclaim your sense of agency.

Forgiveness plays a pivotal role in the process of closure and healing. It's all about releasing resentment and anger towards those who may have overstepped their boundaries or caused unintentional harm. For many, forgiving trusted adults who were not spiritually aware themselves involves understanding that their actions were influenced by their own limitations, conditioning, or lack of awareness. Now, distinguishing between individuals who had malicious intent and those who acted out of ignorance or misguided beliefs is essential. It requires discernment and compassion. People who are spiritually unaware may project their own insecurities or unresolved issues onto others because they are simply unaware of the impact of their actions. Forgiving them does not excuse their behavior but acknowledges their humanity and the complexities of their own spiritual journeys. Plus, forgiveness is an act for you, not them.

Moreover, finding closure involves nurturing self-compassion and self-forgiveness. Try to recognize that you deserve healing and peace, regardless of the circumstances that led to your pain. This process empowers you to reclaim your narrative and define your spiritual path on your terms. It frees you from the shadows of past traumas.

In the end, healing from emotional wounds caused by trusted adults requires creating healthy boundaries and practicing self-care.

Letting the Past Inform the Future

Our past can be painful in hindsight, but it's important for us to reflect on it. Learning history, whether in school or through personal reflection, serves a dual purpose: to glean insights from the past and to apply those lessons to our present and future. Just as we study historical events to understand how societies have navigated challenges and advancements, we can also learn from our own personal histories. Reflecting on our past experiences, especially those marked by pain or difficulty, offers a wonderful opportunity for growth and self-discovery.

When we encounter painful memories or challenging experiences from our past, it can be tempting to bury them or push them aside. However, embracing a mindset that seeks to find the diamond in the rubble encourages us to extract valuable lessons and insights even from the most challenging situations. But finding the diamond in the rubble of past pain involves viewing our experiences with a non-biased lens as much as possible. This requires setting aside preconceived notions, biases, and judgments that may cloud our perception. It entails approaching our memories and emotions with openness and curiosity as we seek to understand the underlying meanings they hold.

Why should you strive to find the lesson in past pain?

Firstly, because every experience (even the most painful ones) has the potential to teach us something valuable about ourselves and the world around us. By confronting and processing past pain, we gain a deeper understanding of our strengths and weaknesses. Secondly, finding meaning in past experiences allows us to integrate those lessons into our present lives. Just as historical knowledge informs decisions and actions in the broader context of society, personal insights gained from past challenges can guide us in making wiser choices and cultivating healthier relationships.

Moreover, embracing a mindset of learning from the past promotes emotional healing and growth. Instead of being weighed down by unresolved pain or bitterness, actively seeking lessons from past experiences empowers us to transform adversity into opportunity. It helps us develop a sense of empowerment and self-awareness, thus, paving the way for personal development and inner peace. However, viewing our past with a non-biased lens is not always easy. Emotions, ingrained beliefs, and subconscious biases can color our perceptions. It requires practice and self-reflection to cultivate a balanced perspective. You'll learn how to do this soon.

*

As you learn to use your hindsight to carve out a more stable spiritual experience for yourself, you will find more meaning in the everyday things that you once took for granted. Even something as simple as a quick catch-up with a good friend will have as much of a restorative effect on you as a full day's worth of interaction. As you deepen your connection to yourself and all of the experiences that have shaped who you are, you will find it easier to embrace your present.

CHAPTER 3 –
EMBRACING YOUR PRESENT

Living in the now is something that not many of us have the ability to do. We often find ourselves plagued by the ghosts of our past or terrified by the prospects of our futures. As you'll have dealt with your past, it's important that we work on your present life.

However, as I've just mentioned, this is not always easy.

Before we get into the finer details, I would like to invite you to come on a mental walk with me. Picture yourself in your mind's eye. Picture yourself at your happiest moment. Think of what you were doing and who you were with. More importantly, think of the person you were being.

That moment in time is when you were most present and the reason why your mind often wanders to that memory is that it was one time in your life when you were completely in "the now." Ultimately, this meant that you were swept up in the present —

there was nothing behind you and nothing ahead of you. While it's important to use your past as a point of reference — and to plan for your future — it's even more crucial to live in the moment. That is because we don't know when our time will be up. Moreover, we don't know what the future will hold for us. There is always the possibility that this is as good as it's ever going to get.

You can let that riddle you with fear.

Or you can choose to make it the best moment... yet.

The Concept of Time

Time, as a concept, has fascinated philosophers, physicists, and thinkers throughout history. This fascination has led to various theories that attempt to explain its nature and implications. From ancient times to modern theories in physics, understanding time involves exploring different perspectives that challenge our intuitive understanding of its passage.

One of the earliest theories of time comes from ancient Greece, where philosophers like Heraclitus proposed that "everything flows" or "panta rhei." This suggests a dynamic and ever-changing reality where nothing remains constant. This view emphasizes the fluidity of time, where the present moment is constantly in flux and the past and future are interconnected in a continuous stream. In contrast, Newtonian physics presented time as an absolute and uniform entity that flows at a constant rate — independent of the observer or the events occurring within it. This classical view of time prevailed for centuries until Einstein's theory of relativity revolutionized our understanding. This theory introduced the concept of spacetime, where time and space are intertwined into a single continuum affected by gravity and motion. According to relativity, time is not uniform but relative to the observer's frame of reference and the gravitational fields they are in. This theory implies that time can slow down or speed up depending on the speed of an object and the gravitational potential it experiences.

Then we have quantum mechanics, which further complicates the picture by suggesting that at the most fundamental levels, time may not be as linear and straightforward as we perceive it. Quantum entanglement, for instance, implies instantaneous connections between particles regardless of the distance between them. This challenges our conventional understanding of causality and temporal sequence. Next, there is string theory (as well as other theories in theoretical physics) that proposes that time may be multidimensional or exist in parallel universes. These concepts speculate that every possible outcome and variation of events may exist simultaneously in a vast "multiverse," where time unfolds in different directions and dimensions.

But these are scientific in nature. From a philosophical standpoint, existentialists like Jean-Paul Sartre and Martin Heidegger contemplated the subjective experience of time and emphasized how human consciousness perceives and constructs temporal reality. Sartre, for example, argued that time is a product of human consciousness and our awareness of mortality, thus influencing how we live and make decisions.

The long and short of it is that time is not at all what we perceive it to be.

Bringing these theories together offers a perspective on the meaning of time in human life. If time is not a linear progression but a multidimensional, interconnected web where past, present, and future coexist, it invites us to reconsider our relationship with the passage of time. This perspective suggests that dwelling excessively on the past or anxiously anticipating the future may be futile. Instead, embracing the present moment becomes crucial as we recognize that all moments — past, present, and future — are interconnected and part of a larger whole. It encourages a shift from a linear, deterministic view of life to one that acknowledges the simultaneity and interconnectedness of all experiences.

In practical terms, this understanding of time invites us to let go of regrets about the past and anxieties about the future. It encourages us to focus, instead, on living fully in the present. It encourages mindfulness, gratitude, and a deeper appreciation for the richness of each moment. Again, the "how" of all of this is for later in the book. At this juncture, what you can begin doing is (re)learning how to love you.

Learning to Love You Now

Learning to love yourself unconditionally is a transformative and rebellious act in a world that profits off your self-loathing. It challenges societal norms and personal insecurities. Often, we're conditioned to believe that self-love hinges on achieving certain standards — being thinner, smarter, or even kinder. However, genuine self-love begins with accepting and appreciating who you are in the present moment.

Society bombards us with ideals of perfection that perpetuate the notion that our worth is tied to external achievements or attributes. This external validation can lead to self-criticism and dissatisfaction, thus, creating the belief that we're not deserving of love until we meet unrealistic standards. Yet, true self-love lies in embracing your inherent value as an individual, irrespective of societal expectations or perceived flaws.

Learning to love yourself now means recognizing that this moment is all you truly have. It involves acknowledging your strengths and weaknesses with compassion and understanding. It requires letting go of the relentless pursuit of an idealized self-image and embracing authenticity and vulnerability instead. Moreover, loving yourself now entails cultivating a positive and nurturing relationship with yourself. It means treating yourself with kindness, patience, and respect. These are qualities that I'm willing to be that you readily extend to others but often withhold from yourself. This shift in mindset allows you to celebrate your accomplishments and forgive yourself for your mistakes.

At its core, loving yourself also involves reframing your perspective on personal growth and development. Instead of viewing self-improvement as a means to attain self-love, it becomes a journey of self-discovery and self-acceptance. It means embracing the idea that you are a constantly evolving being who is worthy of love and acceptance at every stage of your journey. It challenges the pervasive belief that your worthiness is contingent upon external validation or comparison to others. It encourages you to celebrate your uniqueness and individuality by making you recognize that true beauty and worthiness emanate from within.

In a world that often prioritizes achievement over authenticity, practicing self-love demands courage and resilience. It entails letting go of self-limiting beliefs and embracing a mindset of abundance and self-compassion. It involves setting boundaries that honor your needs and values as well as prioritizing self-care and surrounding yourself with people who uplift you.

Ultimately, learning to love yourself in the present moment instead of waiting until you are "more worthy" (which you already are) is a radical act of self-empowerment. Do it!

Balancing Responsibilities with Inner Peace

Of course, when it comes to living in the present moment and loving yourself right this minute, you will have to learn how to balance your responsibilities with inner peace. This is a delicate dance in the modern world where demands often overshadow personal well-being. It's easy to get caught up in the hustle and bustle of daily life — meeting deadlines, fulfilling obligations, and navigating relationships — that the essence of inner peace can become obscured. However, amidst these responsibilities, it's crucial to remember that life is not solely about work and obligations.

Your soul's journey on this earth transcends mere survival and productivity. It yearns for fulfillment, growth, and moments of serenity that nourish the spirit. While work and deadlines are inevitable aspects of life, they need not define your entire existence. They are, in essence, exchanges of energy within the larger mechanism of society, where your contribution is valued and compensated. But it's understandable to feel disheartened or frustrated at times, especially when work seems to consume the majority of your time and energy. However, viewing your role in the workforce as a means to support your life goals — both personal and professional — can shift your perspective. Rather than resenting the demands placed upon you, consider them as opportunities to hone your skills, contribute to a greater purpose, and earn resources that enable a more fulfilling life.

Finding inner peace amidst responsibilities involves cultivating mindfulness and self-awareness. It's about recognizing when you need to pause, recharge, and reconnect with yourself amidst the busyness of life. This may entail setting boundaries, prioritizing self-care, and carving out moments for reflection and rejuvenation. Moreover, reframing your mindset can transform how you perceive and navigate your responsibilities. Instead of viewing work as a hindrance to your peace, see it as a platform for personal growth and contribution. Align your daily actions with your values and aspirations by integrating moments of joy, creativity, and fulfillment into your routine.

Ultimately, harnessing the motivation derived from understanding the transient nature of time and the importance of living authentically can fuel your journey toward balancing responsibilities with inner peace. Try to embrace the realization that life is a web of experiences in which work is just one thread. By nurturing your spiritual and emotional well-being alongside your professional endeavors, you create a harmonious blend of purpose and serenity. However, in the end, balancing responsibilities with inner peace requires intentional choices and a commitment to self-care. Always try to remember to honor your needs as a priority.

*

I understand that being present all of the time will be borderline impossible. In life, there must always be balance and, for us humans, we must have a balance between past, present, and future. Without it, we would be crushed under the sorrow of yesterday or the expectations of tomorrow. Still, the scales must always lean a little more in favor of the present because that is precisely where we are. A moment is lost in the sands of time just as soon as it is experienced. Always remember that.

Part II: Getting to the Core

CHAPTER 4 –

IDENTIFYING CORE VALUES

Once you have a more solid sense of self, getting to the core of who you are will be that much easier. It should go without saying, but you cannot determine what is of value to you without knowing who you truly are. After all, what is of value to you might not be of value to your mother, or your sister, or your best friend, or your neighbor.

So, with that sense of self in mind, it's imperative that you begin unpacking your values. The reason for this is that even without a definitive spiritual path, your values can help you tap into and serve the greater good. And we could all do with the desire (and the means) to contribute to the greater good. After all, if we each did this, the world would be a more idyllic place.

Without proposing that we could deliver on the idea of Elysium in our lifetimes, there is the possibility that we could create a life of paradise within ourselves. But for this to come to fruition, we first need to begin with the core of who we are when no one else is looking.

Defining Personal Core Values

Personal values are the bedrock of who you are and are distinct from mere belief systems which are often influenced by external factors such as culture, religion, or societal norms. They constitute the fundamental principles and ideals that guide your decisions and actions as well as your interactions with the world. Unlike beliefs that can change over time or vary in significance, personal values are deeply ingrained and reflect your authentic self.

Defining your personal values begins with introspection and reflection on what matters most to you. It involves identifying core principles that resonate with your sense of identity, purpose, and integrity. While beliefs can be influenced by external factors, values originate from within and shape your character. They also define the boundaries of your ethical compass.

To define your personal values, start by examining experiences that have shaped your worldview and influenced your priorities. Think back to moments in your life when you felt most fulfilled, proud, or aligned with your truest inner self. These instances often reveal underlying values such as honesty, compassion, perseverance, or creativity that you hold dear. Furthermore, assess how you prioritize different aspects of life — whether it's relationships, career, personal growth, or community involvement. Your values serve as guiding principles that help you make decisions aligned with your aspirations and ethical standards. They provide clarity during challenging times and serve as a moral framework for navigating life's complexities.

It's essential to differentiate personal values from external expectations or societal pressures. Clarifying your personal values will require you to articulate them in concrete terms that resonate with your sense of identity and integrity. Consider qualities or principles that consistently drive your actions and decisions, regardless of external circumstances or opinions. Whether it's integrity, empathy, resilience, or justice, your values shape your priorities and define your approach to life's challenges and opportunities. But defining personal values requires ongoing self-awareness and introspection. As you evolve and grow, your values may evolve as well to reflect new insights, experiences, or aspirations. Embrace this evolution as a natural part of personal development. Allow your values to guide you toward greater authenticity and fulfillment.

Ultimately, personal values are the compass that directs your journey towards self-actualization and meaningful living. If you allow them to take the wheel and you live by them wholeheartedly, you will find that your sense of meaning in life increases. It all boils down to prioritizing what truly matters to you.

Identifying & Prioritizing What Truly Matters

Understanding what is most important to you is foundational in shaping your personal values. Remember that your values are a set of guiding principles that define who you are and how you navigate life. When you want to prioritize your values, you should begin by reflecting on experiences and moments in your life that have brought you a sense of meaning, as previously mentioned. These can be achievements, relationships, or situations where you felt deeply aligned with who you are. Pay attention to the underlying principles or qualities that were present in these experiences. They might include integrity, compassion, growth, creativity, authenticity, justice, or other core values that resonate with you on a deep level. The reason why this is important is that understanding and defining your values will heighten your relationship with yourself. This, in turn, can deepen your spiritual side and your sense of meaning. Of course, this is an ongoing process of self-discovery. By identifying what matters most to you, you lay the groundwork for creating a list of values that accurately reflect your authentic self.

Once you have identified your values, the next step is integrating them into your daily life and decision-making processes. Your values should serve as a reliable compass that guides your actions and choices in various life situations. I encourage you to consider which ones are non-negotiable and hold the greatest significance in shaping your life. Consider creating a hierarchy of values, where you rank them based on their importance and relevance to different aspects of your life. This helps you make decisions that align with your core beliefs and aspirations.

There is a crucial reason for this. When your values clash with external pressures — from parents, partners, employers, or societal expectations — it can evoke a range of emotions. You may experience inner conflict, frustration, or discomfort when asked to engage in activities or behaviors that go against your values. This conflict arises because your values represent what you hold dear and what you think of yourself. To navigate conflicting situations, try to do so with self-awareness and assertiveness. Clearly communicate your values to others and respectfully set boundaries to protect what matters to you. But more importantly, use these moments as opportunities for self-reflection and growth. Assess whether compromising your values aligns with your long-term well-being and goals. I'm fairly sure the answer to that will be a "no" and at that point, you will have no way forward but to align your actions with those values.

Aligning Actions & Decisions

Aligning your decisions and actions with your core values, such as honesty, is pivotal for leading a life of integrity and authenticity. When your values guide your behavior, they serve as a moral compass, influencing how you interact with others and navigate various situations. Let's look at this from a hypothetical standpoint.

Imagine you work for a company where transparency and honesty are core values. One day, you discover discrepancies in the financial records that suggest potential fraud. As someone committed to honesty, you face a moral dilemma. You realize that confronting this issue could jeopardize your relationship with your colleagues and may even affect your job security. However, ignoring the problem goes against your personal values and the company's stated principles.

In this scenario, aligning your decision and actions with the value of honesty involves several steps:

1. **Assessment and Reflection**: Take time to assess the situation objectively. Reflect on the potential consequences of your actions and consider how they align with your personal values and the values of the organization.

2. **Courageous Communication**: Approach the appropriate authorities or supervisors to discuss your concerns in a respectful and professional manner. Express your commitment to honesty and transparency while seeking guidance on how to address the issue effectively.

3. **Integrity in Action**: Act with integrity by adhering to ethical standards and protocols in handling the situation. Follow through on your commitment to honesty, even if it means facing uncomfortable conversations or making difficult decisions.

4. **Impact and Resolution**: Your actions may lead to uncovering the truth and addressing the discrepancies appropriately. While the outcome may involve challenging repercussions, such as confronting wrongdoing or implementing corrective measures, staying true to your values reinforces your integrity and trustworthiness.

You see, aligning decisions with values like honesty can present challenges. You may find yourself navigating conflicts of interest or facing resistance from others who have different priorities. It requires courage and resilience to uphold your principles in the face of adversity. However, these challenges also offer opportunities for personal growth and self-discovery.

*

When all is said and done, the person that you are when no one is around to judge you is the person that dictates your life path. You cannot connect to a force for good that is greater than you if you are insistent on driving it away from you. Yes, religion is a form of spirituality. Yes, some religious texts state that there is forgiveness for ill deeds. But be wary of the idea that you can pray your so-called sins away. At some point, you must acknowledge where you have gone astray and how this deviation from your values impacts your propensity for spiritual connection.

CHAPTER 5 –

EXPLORING PERSONAL BELIEFS

Beyond core values are your core beliefs. These can stem, in part, from your core values, but they are more closely related to your upbringing and your experiences. The sad reality is that many of us grow up with belief systems that are only meant to serve the people who imposed them on us. And because of this, we might experience conflicts (whether consciously or subconsciously) that have us acting out of character. The worst part of all of this is that when you find yourself acting out of character in this way, you may very well push yourself further away from your sense of purpose and meaning.

Ultimately, we all want to have belief systems that help us stay the course with regard to what we deem valuable or meaningful. We want to have belief systems that add to our lives in a purposeful and, perhaps, even spiritual way. The last thing we want is to have belief systems that detract from those very aspects of our lives. For this, we need to reflect.

Examining Personal Beliefs

Previously, we explored the concept of values. Now, let's delve into beliefs, which are another important part of our worldview. While values are principles or standards that shape our behavior and interactions, beliefs are deeply held convictions or opinions about the world, ourselves, and others. Beliefs are often influenced by our upbringing, culture, experiences, and personal interpretations of events.

Examining your personal belief systems requires looking closely at where they come from and how they've shaped who you are. Our beliefs are like the lenses through which we see the world and they influence everything from our decisions and behaviors to our interactions with others. Understanding where these beliefs originated and how they have been reinforced or challenged over time is crucial for gaining a deeper understanding of ourselves.

As mentioned, beliefs develop over time through various influences. Our family and upbringing play a significant role by instilling early beliefs about religion, morality, and social norms in us. These early experiences lay the foundation for many of our core beliefs. As we grow, cultural and societal influences shape our perspectives further. The media we consume, the education we receive, and the societal norms we are exposed to all contribute to the beliefs we hold.

Personal experiences and trauma also play a crucial role in shaping our beliefs. Significant life events, whether they are moments of great joy or deep sorrow, have a major impact on how we see the world. For instance, overcoming a major challenge might strengthen beliefs in resilience and capability, while traumatic experiences might instill beliefs about fear and safety. Then, education and learning introduce us to new ideas and perspectives that often challenge and expand our existing belief systems. Philosophical teachings, scientific discoveries, and academic knowledge can radically alter our views and beliefs.

But from there, engaging in critical thinking and self-reflection is essential for examining your beliefs. It allows you to question their validity and consider their origins. Are they truly your own or have they been imposed upon you by external influences? Reflecting on the consistency of your beliefs across different areas of your life can reveal contradictions or areas where your beliefs may no longer serve you. This self-examination encourages you to challenge assumptions and consider alternative viewpoints. Essentially, this has the propensity to encourage intellectual growth and personal development.

The thing to remember here is that our beliefs can impact our behavior and well-being whether we'd like them to or not. They shape how we interpret events, form judgments, and react to challenges. Positive beliefs can empower us — boosting our confidence and resilience, while negative beliefs can limit our potential and contribute to feelings of self-doubt or anxiety. Ultimately, this process of introspection and growth is essential for living a life that is true to yourself and free from the constraints of limiting beliefs. It opens you up to the possibilities of personal transformation. If you can withstand the discomfort for long enough, you can carve away at some inherited beliefs — if not all of them.

Inherited Beliefs & Societal Norms

In the previous section, we explored how inherited beliefs and societal norms contribute to shaping our identities and influencing our behaviors within various contexts of life. Now, we delve deeper into understanding the impact of these influences on our personal growth, relationships, and overall well-being. Essentially, inherited beliefs are deeply rooted convictions passed down through generations within families and cultural communities. They encompass traditions and moral principles that shape our worldview as well as our sense of identity from an early age. These beliefs provide a framework for understanding the world and navigating personal and social interactions.

Societal norms, on the other hand, are the unwritten rules and expectations that define acceptable behavior and roles within a particular community or society. These norms govern everything from social etiquette and communication styles to gender roles, family dynamics, and professional conduct. Adhering to societal norms often allows for social cohesion and predictability but can also constrain individual expression and diversity.

But what are their spectrums of influence?

Well, the influence of inherited beliefs and societal norms extends across various facets of life. First off, inherited beliefs contribute significantly to our sense of identity and self-perception. They provide a cultural and moral compass that guides our understanding of right and wrong. This foundation shapes how we define ourselves and perceive our place within our family, community, and society at large. From there, societal norms usually dictate behavioral expectations in social, familial, and professional settings. They define appropriate conduct, communication styles, and roles based on cultural expectations and traditions. At the same time, these elements play a crucial role in shaping social dynamics and relationships. They establish norms for interpersonal interactions, family structures, and community engagement. Relationships are often influenced by shared beliefs and values, while conflicts may arise when individual beliefs diverge from societal expectations.

Over time, inherited beliefs and societal norms evolve in response to cultural, political, and social changes. Cultural evolution reflects shifts in attitudes and societal priorities, but hardly ever individual values. And that's the problem.

To move through this difficult period of transformation, it's advised that you not only engage in critical reflection but also develop emotional awareness. When you acknowledge and validate your emotions when navigating conflicts between personal beliefs and societal expectations, you reaffirm the worth of your values. It's also important to develop cultural competence by actively engaging with diverse perspectives and experiences. When you're carving out your own beliefs, it's crucial that you stave off the temptation to judge those who judge you. Instead, engage in empathy and understanding for differing beliefs and cultural practices — even those that might have previously held you back. Respectfully navigate cultural differences and promote inclusive dialogue to encourage mutual respect and collaboration.

This is how you will empower yourself to redefine and prioritize beliefs that resonate with your authentic self. Embrace opportunities for personal growth, self-expression, and fulfillment, even in the face of societal pressures or expectations. If need be, form your own belief system.

Forming Your Own Belief System

Forming your own belief system is not merely a matter of personal preference. It is an essential journey towards spiritual fulfillment and authenticity. It entails delving deep into your values and experiences as well as your understanding of the world. Doing this will allow you to construct a framework that resonates genuinely with your inner self.

When you form your own belief system, you walk the path of self-discovery and self-definition. It allows you to break away from inherited beliefs or societal norms that may not align with your true values and aspirations. This process is crucial for developing a sense of autonomy and personal agency in shaping your life's direction. At its core, forming your own belief system is about spiritual growth and authenticity. It involves questioning inherited beliefs and societal norms to discern what truly resonates with your soul. By aligning your beliefs with your inner truth, you cultivate a deeper connection with yourself and the world around you. This authenticity creates inner peace, clarity of purpose, and a heightened sense of spiritual well-being.

So, how do you do this?

Firstly, solitude is often necessary to form your own belief system effectively. Just as the prodigal son ventured into the world to gain perspective on his values and return home with newfound wisdom, isolating yourself from external influences allows for introspection and self-discovery. It provides the space to examine your beliefs, values, and experiences without external distractions or pressures. But the parable of the prodigal son also exemplifies the journey of self-discovery and spiritual renewal through solitude. The son leaves his father's home in search of independence and worldly experiences, only to realize that true fulfillment lies in aligning with his father's values and returning home. This narrative illustrates the transformative power of introspection and solitude in reaffirming one's beliefs and values.

Ultimately, only you know whether or not your old beliefs align with your values and the spiritual being you want to become. You may very well go through this entire book only to find that you need to be doing more of what you already are. And that is perfectly fine!

But I digress.

Isolation enables you to reconnect with your authentic beliefs and values that may have been overshadowed or diluted by external influences. It offers the opportunity to discern which beliefs resonate genuinely with your inner truth and which no longer serve your spiritual growth. Through introspection and reflection, you gain clarity on what beliefs align with your values, aspirations, and vision for a meaningful life. Just keep in mind that forming your own belief system is not a static process but a dynamic journey of personal evolution. It involves openness to new ideas, experiences, and perspectives that contribute to your spiritual growth and understanding. Embracing change and adaptation allows your belief system to evolve organically as you gain new insights and wisdom throughout your life's journey.

At the end of the day, this journey toward spiritual authenticity will enrich your relationships and enhance your resilience in facing life's challenges. Don't allow the fear of losing an old belief system (or really committing to it) to stop you.

*

With solid personal beliefs that add value to your life as opposed to taking from it, you can begin to tap back into your emotional center. This will be a paramount next step because, with your emotions offline, you cannot truly gauge what is meant for you and what isn't. Moreover, as you get to grips with old personal beliefs that no longer serve, you might need to go through several emotions before you can process the old and make space for the new.

CHAPTER 6 –

BUILDING EMOTIONAL RESILIENCE

Our emotions have the ability to control our lives as well as our connection to our higher selves. When you're on a quest for meaning, you'll want to ensure that you can keep these emotions in check. Now, this does not necessarily mean that you should suppress your emotions. In fact, it means the opposite. What I mean by this is that you should experience and express your emotions in a healthy manner.

The reason why I say this is that we do not build emotional resilience by avoiding our emotions. We build emotional resilience by facing them and searching for the meaning within them. What was our anger trying to protect us from when it poured out our mouths like hot lava? What was our sadness signaling that we needed relief from when it tumbled from our eyes like hot waterfalls?

All of this matters because it is how we will find that sense of meaning and connection to our spiritual centers.

Understanding Emotional Resilience

Now it's time for us to understand emotional resilience. This is a vital quality that empowers individuals to navigate life's challenges with adaptability, strength, and a sense of inner balance. It encompasses the capacity to withstand adversity, recover from setbacks, and maintain mental well-being amid stressors. Understanding and cultivating emotional resilience is crucial in creating a bedrock for your mental health as well as in promoting personal growth and enhancing overall quality of life.

But what is it?

Simply put, it is the ability to bounce back from difficult experiences, adversity, or trauma. It involves maintaining a sense of perspective during crises. Resilient individuals demonstrate flexibility in their thinking and maintain a positive outlook. They possess strong coping mechanisms that help them navigate life's ups and downs with greater ease.

To help you understand this further, I've created a list of the components of emotional resilience on the next page.

1. **Self-Awareness and Emotional Regulation**: Emotional resilience begins with self-awareness – the ability to recognize and understand your emotions, strengths, and limitations. By developing emotional regulation skills, you can manage intense emotions and stressors effectively.

2. **Adaptability and Flexibility**: Resilient individuals demonstrate adaptability in response to changing circumstances and challenges. They are open to new perspectives, willing to learn from setbacks, and able to adjust their goals (as well as strategies) as needed to achieve positive outcomes.

3. **Optimism and Positive Mindset**: Maintaining a positive outlook creates emotional resilience by enabling you to see setbacks as temporary and opportunities for growth. Optimistic thinking helps in reframing challenges as manageable and encourages perseverance in achieving long-term goals.

4. **Supportive Relationships**: Strong social connections and support networks play a crucial role in enhancing emotional resilience. Building and nurturing supportive relationships provide emotional validation, practical assistance, and a sense of belonging, which buffer against stress and adversity.

5. **Problem-Solving Skills**: Effective problem-solving skills will also enable you to approach challenges constructively and find practical solutions. Resilient individuals assess situations realistically, break problems down into

manageable parts, and take proactive steps to address issues.

It's important not to underestimate the importance of resilience but it's also important not to allow your setbacks to confuse you. Just because you fall down and cry that doesn't mean you're not resilient. Resilience is not defined by the fall. It is defined by how you get up. So, don't beat yourself up for having normal human emotions. Have those emotions and then get up with more fervor than before.

Strategies for Developing Resilience & Coping with Stress

To do this, you will need to develop and hone skills and practices that promote mental well-being. You will also need to enhance your coping mechanisms and develop a more positive outlook. Prioritizing self-care is foundational to building emotional resilience. **Adequate sleep, proper nutrition, regular exercise**, and **relaxation techniques** are important aspects of self-care that promote physical and mental well-being. When you prioritize your own needs and health, you build a strong foundation from which to face challenges effectively. Self-care not only replenishes physical energy but also supports emotional regulation and mental clarity, enabling individuals to navigate stressors with greater resilience.

Also, practices such as yoga, meditation, deep breathing exercises, or journaling provide opportunities for introspection as well as emotional processing and stress relief. These activities create a sense of calm and inner peace, thus, allowing you to cultivate a positive mindset and develop effective coping strategies. It's also worth building strong social support networks and seeking professional help when needed. Social support provides emotional validation, practical assistance, and a sense of belonging. Ultimately, this all creates a buffer against stress and adversity. Connecting with trusted friends, family members, or support groups allows you to share experiences and receive empathy during difficult times. Professional support, such as counseling or therapy, offers specialized assistance in developing coping skills. A therapist can help you manage emotions and navigate complex challenges.

Your loved ones can also help you view setbacks as opportunities for learning and growth, which is essential for promoting emotional resilience. Remember that reflecting on past challenges, identifying lessons learned, and applying insights to future situations can enhance coping mechanisms. In learning from experiences, you will develop your emotional intelligence, adaptive problem-solving skills, and a sense of empowerment in overcoming obstacles. What I'd like you to be aware of throughout this process is that coping with stress while cultivating emotional resilience is a holistic endeavor that encompasses various strategies to manage and mitigate the impact of stressors.

With this, you will need to train your mind on how to think positively and find the silver linings in all that occurs in your life.

The Role of Positive Thinking

Positive thinking plays a big role in enhancing your emotional well-being and encouraging spiritual growth. Positive thinking offers transformative benefits across various aspects of life. At its core, positive thinking involves maintaining an optimistic outlook by focusing on constructive thoughts. Positive thinking focuses more on solving the problem than the actual problem itself.

Emotional well-being and spirituality are intricately linked to positive thinking because they influence how you perceive and respond to certain circumstances. Optimistic attitudes contribute to lower levels of stress, anxiety, and depression by promoting a sense of hope, optimism, and emotional balance. When faced with adversity, you can view setbacks as temporary and surmountable, thus, enabling yourself to approach challenges with greater confidence and resilience.

Spiritual growth also thrives in the soil of positive thinking. It encourages you to explore deeper meanings and connections within yourself and the world around you. In this regard, positive thinking creates a sense of gratitude, compassion, and acceptance, which are fundamental to spiritual practices and beliefs. By cultivating an optimistic mindset, you can align your thoughts and actions with spiritual values such as love, forgiveness, and inner peace, thereby deepening your spiritual journey. This will feed into your personal growth and self-improvement because you will be empowered to identify and leverage your strengths as well as to pursue goals with determination and overcome self-limiting beliefs. By focusing on possibilities and opportunities, positive thinking fuels motivation and creativity, thus, enabling you to explore new perspectives and solutions to challenges that may come up along the way.

But practicing positive thinking will call for you to develop self-awareness, which we discussed earlier. It requires you to observe your thoughts and consciously choose to reframe negative or pessimistic thinking patterns into more optimistic and empowering ones. Techniques such as affirmations, visualization, and gratitude exercises are effective tools for cultivating positive thinking habits and nurturing emotional well-being. This will lend itself to your relationships, where positive thinking can contribute to healthier interactions and deeper connections. Do your best to move with optimism because that manner of being will help you approach others with empathy and kindness.

I'd like to leave you with an example before we move on to the next section. This is the story of — let's call her — Maya.

Maya was a young graphic designer passionate about creating art that spoke to the soul. Fresh out of college, she landed a job at a prestigious design firm. Initially, everything seemed perfect. Maya's creativity flowed and her projects received praise from colleagues. However, months later, setbacks began testing her emotional resilience. The first major setback came when a project she worked on tirelessly for weeks was abruptly canceled due to budget cuts. The project was close to her heart and she had poured her creativity as well as all of her energy into it. When she received the news, Maya felt a wave of disappointment and frustration. Initially, she didn't handle it well. She internalized the failure and felt like it was a reflection of her worth and abilities. She thought that maybe if she had worked harder, the project would have been seen as more valuable, and it wouldn't have been the first to get the cut.

Soon after, Maya faced another blow. Her direct supervisor, who was a mentor and advocate for her, left the company. The new supervisor was a demanding and critical figure. He did not appreciate Maya's artistic style. This created a stressful work environment for her. She started receiving negative feedback, further eroding her confidence. Maya often worked overtime in a bid to try to meet unrealistic expectations. She felt constantly on edge.

Maya was floundering and she knew that something had to change. Over time, Maya developed positive coping strategies. She took up yoga to manage her stress and began painting again to reconnect with her passion for art. These activities provided a sense of calm and allowed her to express herself creatively outside of work. She also sought support from a therapist, who helped her build tools for emotional regulation. But her real turning point came when she decided to have an open conversation with her new supervisor. She respectfully explained her artistic vision and how it aligned with the company's goals. While the supervisor's response was not entirely positive, Maya felt empowered for standing up for herself. She realized that advocating for her beliefs and maintaining her integrity were crucial components of emotional resilience.

And you can do the same. When you approach difficult situations with your values in mind, it won't make the situations any less difficult. However, it will at least give you the peace of mind of knowing that you haven't compromised on what is important to you.

*

We've reached the end of Part II, but we are only beginning the practical side of this book. At this point, we will begin with more practical paths to helping you be present and find meaning in your daily life. Before you dive into that section, keep in mind that your emotional resilience will be needed on a daily basis. You will encounter difficult situations throughout your life and it will be up to your sense of spiritual stability to help you navigate through it.

Part III: Practical Paths for the Present

CHAPTER 7 –

CONNECTING WITH OTHERS

In your pursuit of meaning, how you engage with people around you will shape the outcome of your overall success on this path. We, as human beings, are born with an inherent need for connection. From the moment we are conceived, we rely on the womb of another for survival. Then, we require her embrace to comfort and nurture us. From there, we require others our age to socialize with us. And, finally, we need companions of some sort for the rest of our lives. When we start businesses, it is to serve others. We work for organizations and have colleagues. We pursue academia and have peers and supervisors who review our research.

All throughout our lives, we are connected to another living being in some way, shape, or form.

Therefore, it makes sense that our connection with others could help us find a deepened sense of meaning. From a spiritual standpoint, our interconnectedness is a reminder of our connection to something greater than ourselves — some invisible web that weaves each of our lives together.

The Importance of Building Healthy Relationships

Building healthy relationships is vital to our emotional well-being and spiritual journey because they shape the way we perceive ourselves, others, and the world around us. Essentially, healthy relationships provide us with a sense of belonging, support, and connection that nourishes our souls and enhances our overall quality of life.

One of the fundamental aspects of healthy relationships is their role in creating emotional resilience and well-being. When we engage in supportive and loving relationships, we experience emotional validation that helps us feel more confident in our own actions. It also provides us with a sense of acceptance and "oneness" that we crave as human beings. This elevates the amount of empathy that we give to others and receive from them in return. These positive interactions contribute to our sense of self-worth and confidence, thus, reinforcing a positive self-image and helping us navigate challenges with greater ease.

From a spiritual perspective, healthy relationships are essential because they reflect our capacity to embody values such as love, compassion, and forgiveness. Through our interactions with others, we practice empathy, kindness, and generosity. These are central tenets of many spiritual traditions. These connections deepen our understanding of interconnectedness and the universal human experience, thus, giving us a sense of unity and harmony in our spiritual journey. However, ***unhealthy*** relationships can hinder our spiritual growth and emotional well-being. Toxic dynamics characterized by manipulation, control, or a lack of trust can erode our self-esteem and inner peace. People will take up space in our heads virtually rent-free and we'll find ourselves descending into angry thoughts that are fueled by our desire to stand up for ourselves. In the long run, such relationships may prevent us from expressing our authentic selves or pursuing our aspirations. This can lead to emotional distress and spiritual stagnation.

Needless to say, we need to build healthy relationships and this requires mutual respect, open communication, and a willingness to cultivate trust as well as intimacy over time. These qualities create a supportive environment where individuals feel safe to express their thoughts, emotions, and vulnerabilities without fear of judgment or rejection. In turn, healthy relationships promote personal growth and a deeper connection to our spiritual beliefs and values. They contribute to our sense of purpose and fulfillment in life because when we engage in reciprocal and supportive interactions with others, we experience an intense sense of joy, fulfillment, and satisfaction. Shared experiences, celebrations, and mutual support create lasting memories and strengthen the bonds that sustain us during both joyful and challenging times. These moments are golden opportunities for spiritual practice and growth. But this also applies to acts of kindness, forgiveness, and compassion toward others. Through these acts, we cultivate virtues that align with our spiritual beliefs and values.

In essence, the importance of building healthy relationships lies in their ability to nurture our emotional well-being, support our spiritual growth, and enrich our lives with love, connection, and meaning. But to build these relationships, you will need to learn how to communicate effectively.

Effective Communication Skills

Effective communication skills are important in any aspect of life. Relationship-building is no different. That remains the same whether you're talking about personal, professional, or spiritual relationships. Beyond the fundamental aspects of exchanging information and ideas, effective communication encompasses the ability to listen actively, empathize, express oneself authentically, and navigate conflicts constructively. These skills not only enhance the quality of our interactions but also contribute to our overall satisfaction in relationships. Other than the standards, such as active listening and empathy, which I have addressed in other books in this series, we need to do our level best to engage in authentic expression.

Authenticity in communication involves expressing oneself honestly and transparently while respecting the feelings and perspectives of others. It entails sharing thoughts, emotions, and beliefs openly, without pretense or manipulation. I can't stress the importance of authentic communication enough because it builds trust and credibility. It also demonstrates sincerity and integrity in our interactions. When we communicate authentically, we create an environment where vulnerability is welcomed. This allows us to create deeper connections based on mutual understanding and acceptance.

Nonverbal cues such as facial expressions, gestures, posture, and tone of voice, of course, play a significant role in communication. They often convey far more meaning than words could ever do on their own. Effective communicators are mindful of their nonverbal signals to ensure that they align with their verbal messages. You'll need to make an effort to ensure that your nonverbal communication contributes to clarity and coherence in communication. Awareness of nonverbal cues also allows individuals to interpret the emotions and intentions of others more accurately, which can facilitate empathetic responses and enhance connection in interactions.

Not only will all of this help you navigate conflict effectively (conflict which could potentially detract from your spiritual experiences) but it will also help to build rapport and trust. Like many other elements of relationship building, this is a continuous process that relies on effective communication skills. It involves establishing a sense of connection, reliability, and mutual respect with others over time. This is how you can connect to those around you and build a strong sense of community with those who align with your values.

The Role of Community & Support Networks

I'll say it again: human beings are inherently social creatures and the role of community and support networks in encouraging personal and spiritual growth cannot be overstated. At its core, community provides a framework within which we can connect, learn, and evolve. Whether in physical neighborhoods, online forums, or spiritual congregations, these networks offer a multitude of benefits that contribute significantly to your pursuit of meaning. That is because communities offer a sense of belonging that is crucial for personal and spiritual actualization. They provide a platform where people can share their experiences, exchange ideas, and find acceptance without judgment. This sense of connection helps to mitigate feelings of loneliness and isolation, which are often barriers to growth and self-realization.

Just remember that as you begin trying to find your own path, exposing yourself to diverse communities will expose you to a range of perspectives, beliefs, and experiences. This exposure will deepen your sense of empathy because the more you get to experience other people, the more you come to understand them. This has the power to broaden horizons and challenge ingrained biases or limited worldviews. Through interactions with people from different backgrounds and cultures, you'll gain new insights, expand your knowledge, and develop a more nuanced understanding of yourself through the lens of others.

Support networks within communities play a pivotal role in building emotional resilience. During times of adversity or uncertainty, community members can offer practical assistance that will keep you on track. Challenges are called challenges for a reason — they will challenge your ability to stay true to your values if they are intense enough. Everything from the loss of a child to the sudden demise of your income sources can rattle you to the point of self-destruction. But these relationships provide a safety net that helps you navigate these difficult moments with greater strength and perseverance. They can hold you up when you don't feel like it's possible to take one more step. They will keep you going when you are down on your luck. Moreover, they will hold you accountable when you don't even want to think about it. In these types of supportive environments, you will be encouraged to strive for personal improvement and to contribute positively to the community. Whether through mentorship, peer encouragement, or collaborative projects, community engagement encourages you to set higher standards for yourself and uphold ethical principles.

In some cases, your communities could also serve as spiritual hubs where you get to explore and deepen your beliefs. And this isn't just limited to religious congregations. Meditation groups or philosophical circles offer rituals, teachings, and practices that nurture spiritual growth. These gatherings provide opportunities for reflection, prayer, or meditation, which can help you establish a deeper connection with your spirituality. They can help you set the stage for becoming more mindful in your everyday life.

*

These connections with others will continue to shape your connection to yourself. As they do, you will find that you are able to recognize the relationships that feed your soul and those that dampen your energy. While I don't encourage you to cut people off unnecessarily or to judge people too harshly, I do encourage you to prioritize the connections that matter the most to you. This is your journey and some people are only meant to enter your life for a season — perhaps to teach you some type of lesson or to show you something about yourself.

CHAPTER 8 –

MERGING INTO MINDFUL PRACTICES

This subject has been brought up throughout my book series and for good reason — far too many of us find it virtually impossible to slow down and experience the present moment. Because of this, we're not mindful. We're not mindful when we speak to people we claim to care about. We're not mindful of our actions. We're not mindful of what we put into our bodies in the form of energy, food, and the media.

We're mind*less*.

And because we're mindless, we're unable to enjoy the present moment. But the sad reality is that you might not wake up tomorrow. I know it might sound like an overused book trope — something to rattle your cage and get you to "wake up." But it's the truth. None of us knows when we'll say goodnight to the people we love for the last time. Tomorrow is not guaranteed to anyone and, as such, we have to do our best to make the best of the present moment.

Introduction to Mindfulness

Mindfulness is a cornerstone that I have covered extensively in this series of books and for good reason. It delves deep into the essence of human consciousness and spiritual growth. As a refresher, mindfulness is about cultivating a heightened awareness of the present moment. The act of becoming mindful centers around your thoughts, emotions, and bodily sensations, but also the environment around you. This practice encourages you to engage fully with your inner self and external surroundings without judgment or attachment to the past or future.

Mindfulness originates from ancient contemplative traditions, but it finds its roots primarily in Buddhist teachings and meditation practices. In Buddhist philosophy, mindfulness — known as "sati" in Pali — has been integral to cultivating wisdom and ethical conduct for over two millennia. It emerged as a means to alleviate suffering by developing a clear awareness of mental states and promoting inner peace through meditative practices. But the migration of mindfulness from Eastern spiritual traditions to Western psychology only began in the 20th century. It was spurred by pioneers like Jon Kabat-Zinn. He introduced Mindfulness-Based Stress Reduction (MBSR), which is a secular adaptation that integrates mindfulness into therapeutic settings to alleviate **stress, chronic pain**, and **psychological disorders**. This integration marked a pivotal moment that highlighted mindfulness's potential beyond religious contexts to enhance mental health and spiritual enlightenment amongst diverse populations.

However, mindfulness's true significance lies in its transformative impact on various aspects of our human experiences. Practicing mindfulness facilitates stress reduction by redirecting attention from past regrets or future anxieties to the present moment. It promotes emotional resilience by creating a non-reactive awareness of feelings and thoughts, thus, allowing you to respond thoughtfully rather than impulsively to difficult situations and obstacles. And beyond mental health benefits, mindfulness enhances cognitive functions such as attention, concentration, and memory. By training the mind to focus intentionally, you can improve productivity and decision-making skills. Moreover, mindfulness nurtures self-awareness of your thoughts, emotions, and behaviors. This, in turn, lays the foundation for personal growth and development.

Spiritually, mindfulness serves as a gateway to existential exploration and inner peace. It invites you to contemplate life's deeper questions and connect with a broader sense of purpose and meaning. Through mindfulness practices, you enrich the road to self-discovery with lessons from your inner self — gradually uncovering layers of conditioned habits and beliefs to reveal your authentic self. In essence, mindfulness transcends being a mere psychological technique. It is a way of life that encourages you to embrace each moment with openness, curiosity, and acceptance. By integrating mindfulness into your daily routines and cultivating present-moment awareness, you nurture a sense of spiritual fulfillment. Thus, mindfulness remains a timeless practice that empowers you to live more consciously and harmoniously with yourself and the world around you.

The Benefits of a Regular Mindfulness Routine

There are countless benefits of regular mindfulness practices. First and foremost, mindfulness has the ability to quiet the incessant chatter of the mind. This allows you to observe your thoughts, emotions, and sensations without judgment or attachment. This non-reactive awareness serves as a gateway to understanding the true nature of existence and your place within it. By embracing mindfulness, you go inward in a way that reveals conditioned thoughts and habitual patterns. This can help you get to the core of your authentic self, so if you're struggling in this area, consider starting with this step first.

Essentially, when it's done right, mindfulness encourages introspection and self-inquiry. It helps you to explore your inner landscape with curiosity and compassion. Through regular practice, you develop a clearer understanding of your aspirations and the reasons behind them. Instead of being led to believe that your reason for wanting a large home is simply materialistic, mindfulness could reveal that what you actually crave is security, warmth, comfort, and safety. You can then align your actions with your deepest truths and in accordance with your current means. This is how you'll allow yourself to find meaning even If you're not at the upper echelon of what you perceive to be "financial success." But this is just one example. The essence here is that the process of self-discovery with mindfulness nurtures authenticity, which will provide you with more meaning.

Mindfulness practices, such as **meditation** and **mindful breathing**, promote emotional resilience by enhancing self-regulation and stress management skills. By cultivating a non-judgmental awareness of your thoughts and emotions, you will learn to respond thoughtfully rather than react impulsively to external stimuli. This mindful approach to emotional well-being reduces anxiety, depression, and other mental health concerns. In short, it creates a stable foundation for spiritual growth.

Practical Exercises

I would be remiss not to provide you with an introduction to practical exercises that you can implement in your daily life. Of course, I encourage you to do your own digging on the ones that strike a chord with you. Your interest in one or more will be a good sign that you have found something that can resonate with you on a deeper level. So, without further ado, here they are.

Mindful Breathing

This is one of the easiest (and best) mindfulness practices. All you need to do is take a few moments each day to focus totally on your breathing. Tyr to take note of the sensations you experience as the air enters your body and as the air leaves your body. Feel the rise and fall of your chest as well as the rhythmic nature of your breathing. If your mind wanders to thoughts that make you feel ill at ease, just acknowledge them and gently bring your attention back to your breath.

Body Scan Meditation

The body scan meditation involves paying close attention to different parts of your body, from your toes to the top of your head. This practice helps you connect with your physical sensations and promotes relaxation. Start by lying down or sitting comfortably, and slowly guide your awareness through each part of your body, noting any tension, discomfort, or sensations without judgment.

Mindful Eating

Transform your meals into mindfulness practices by eating mindfully. Pay very close attention to the details, such as the flavors, colors, textures, and smells of your food. Chew slowly and savor each bite, noticing how your body responds to the food. This practice not only enhances your appreciation of food but also promotes healthier eating habits.

Walking Meditation

Walking meditation involves bringing mindfulness to the simple act of walking. Choose a quiet place and walk slowly, paying attention to each step you take. Notice the sensation of your feet touching the ground, the movement of your legs, and the rhythm of your walk. Walking meditation can be done indoors or outdoors and is a great way to combine physical activity with mindfulness.

Mindful Listening

You can practice mindful listening by giving your entire attention to the sounds that are going on around you. Whether it's the sound of birds chirping, the hum of traffic, or a conversation with a friend, focus on truly listening without judgment or distraction. This practice enhances your ability to be present and engaged in your interactions.

Loving-Kindness Meditation

Loving-kindness meditation, also known as Metta meditation, involves cultivating feelings of compassion and love towards yourself and others. Begin by sitting comfortably and focusing on your breath. Then, silently repeat phrases such as "May I be happy, may I be healthy, may I be safe, may I live with ease." Gradually extend these wishes to others, including loved ones, acquaintances, and even people you find challenging.

Mindful Journaling

Take a few minutes each day to journal mindfully. Write down your thoughts, feelings, and experiences without judgment or analysis. This practice helps you process your emotions, gain insights into your inner world, and develop a deeper connection with yourself.

Mindful Technology Use

Incorporate mindfulness into your relationship with technology by setting boundaries and being intentional about your screen time. Take regular breaks from digital devices, practice deep breathing before checking emails or social media, and be fully present during conversations without the distraction of your phone.

Mindful Stretching

Integrate mindfulness into your physical routine by practicing mindful stretching. Pay attention to the sensations in your muscles as you stretch, and focus on your breath as you move through each stretch. This practice can be particularly beneficial in relieving tension and promoting relaxation.

Gratitude Practice

Cultivate a sense of gratitude by regularly reflecting on the things you are thankful for. Take a few moments each day to write down or mentally note three things you are grateful for. This practice helps shift your focus from what is lacking to what is abundant in your life, fostering a positive mindset.

Mindful Observation

Choose an object in your environment, such as a flower, a candle, or a piece of artwork, and spend a few minutes observing it mindfully. Notice its colors, shapes, textures, and any other details. This practice helps you develop a deeper appreciation for the beauty and intricacies of the world around you.

Mindful Bathing

Turn your daily shower or bath into a mindful experience. Pay attention to the sensation of the water on your skin, the temperature, and the sound of the water flowing. Notice the scent of your soap or shampoo and the feeling of lathering it on your body. This practice can transform a routine activity into a calming and centering experience.

Mindful Commuting

If you commute to work, that is a great time to practice mindfulness. Instead of zoning out or getting frustrated by traffic, bring your attention to the present moment. Notice the scenery, the sounds, and the sensations of being in the vehicle. If you take public transportation, observe the people around you and practice mindful breathing.

Mindful Cleaning

Household chores can become opportunities for mindfulness. Whether you're washing dishes, vacuuming, or folding laundry, focus on the physical sensations and movements involved in the task. Notice the texture of the items you're cleaning, the sound of the vacuum, or the rhythm of folding clothes. This practice can help you find peace and satisfaction in routine activities.

Mindful Waiting

Transform periods of waiting into moments of mindfulness. Whether you're waiting in line at the grocery store, at a doctor's office, or for an appointment, use this time to focus on your breath or observe your surroundings without judgment. This practice can help you remain calm and patient in situations that might otherwise be frustrating.

Mindful Gardening

Gardening provides a wonderful opportunity to connect with nature and practice mindfulness. Pay attention to the sensations of your hands in the soil, the smell of the plants, and the sight of your garden growing. Notice the changes in your plants over time and the impact of your care and attention.

Mindful Driving

Practice mindfulness while driving by focusing on the act of driving itself. Notice the sensation of your hands on the steering wheel, the feeling of the car moving, and the sights and sounds around you. Avoid distractions and bring your attention back to the present moment whenever your mind wanders.

Mindful Silence

Set aside time each day to sit in silence. This practice involves simply being present without engaging in any specific activity or distraction. Use this time to observe your thoughts, feelings, and physical sensations without judgment. Mindful silence can help you cultivate inner peace and clarity.

Mindful Creativity

Incorporate mindfulness into creative activities such as painting, drawing, writing, or playing music. Focus on the process of creating rather than the final product. Notice the sensations, thoughts, and emotions that arise as you engage in your creative practice.

Mindful Affirmations

Use affirmations mindfully by repeating positive statements to yourself with full awareness and intention. Choose affirmations that resonate with your values and goals, and take a few moments each day to say them out loud or write them down. This practice can help you cultivate a positive mindset and reinforce your intentions.

*

Once you begin embracing the practice of mindfulness, you will realize just how fast you're spinning in a world that can often distract you from what is most important. Remember that you are a spiritual being having a physical experience. And while you are very much all three aspects — the mind, body, and soul — while you are here, the soul's experience still holds more weight than any other. And what the soul craves is to experience life in the "now."

CHAPTER 9 –

EXPLORING SPIRITUAL PATHS

As your search for meaning gets deeper and deeper, you will find that you are more open to exploring different spiritual paths. While there are countless people who hide behind the veil of false spirituality and try to use that as a means to control others, true spirituality can be incredibly uplifting. The important thing to note here is that spirituality begins from within. Yes, you can align with a certain spiritual teaching or even a religion, but it must first come from within yourself. Your truth is going to be different from the person next to you and their truth will be different from the next person too. This is simply because spirituality is a personal journey.

With that in mind, I would like you to open your heart to the idea of exploring spirituality in a way that is meaningful to you. Find where your energy naturally flows and try not to deviate from the idea of it out of spite of those who wear the veil of fake spirituality. Instead, use those potentially negative experiences to fuel your positive experiences by showing yourself what you do not want to be and what you believe is your path.

Various Spiritual Traditions & Practices

Spiritual practices have evolved and diversified across cultures and time periods. This reflects humanity's quest for meaning, connection, and transcendence. Exploring various ancient, traditional, new age, and modern spiritual practices reveals a rich picture of beliefs and rituals that cater to different needs and contexts. Ancient spiritual practices, for instance, often revolve around the worship of deities, nature, and the cosmos. In ancient Egypt, spirituality was deeply intertwined with daily life and governance. The Egyptians practiced rituals to honor gods like Ra, Osiris, and Isis — believing that these deities controlled the forces of nature and human destiny. Practices included temple rituals, offerings, and elaborate burial ceremonies designed to ensure a safe passage to the afterlife. Similarly, in ancient Greece, spirituality was characterized by polytheism, with gods such as Zeus, Athena, and Apollo. The Greeks believed in the power of these gods to influence human affairs and natural phenomena. Practices included visiting oracles, like the Oracle of Delphi, where individuals sought divine guidance. It also included festivals, like the Olympic Games, which had religious significance and honored Zeus.

Then there are the traditional spiritual practices in indigenous cultures. These often emphasize a connection with nature and ancestral spirits. Native American spirituality, for example, involves rituals such as sweat lodges, vision quests, and powwows. These practices aim to create harmony with the natural world and honor the spirits of ancestors. It is how they seek spiritual guidance and healing. Similarly, in African traditional religions, practices such as drumming, dancing, and libations are performed to communicate with spirits and deities. This is how they maintain social harmony and ensure the community's well-being.

Shortly after traditional religions came to the fore, new-age spirituality emerged in the 20th century. It evolved as a response to the perceived limitations of organized religion and the quest for personal spiritual experiences. It draws on a variety of traditions, including Eastern philosophies, Western esotericism, and indigenous practices. Mindfulness and meditation are fundamental to new-age spirituality. They are often influenced by Buddhist and Hindu practices. Techniques such as mindfulness meditation, transcendental meditation, and guided visualization aim to create inner peace, self-awareness, and spiritual growth. Crystal healing is another popular practice, which is based on the belief that crystals possess healing properties that can balance the body's energy fields.

There are more modern spiritual practices, such as astrology, not to be confused with the ancient practice of astronomy, which involves interpreting the positions and movements of celestial bodies to gather insights into human behavior and even predict the future in some cases. Yoga is another modern pursuit that is actually rooted in ancient Indian traditions. It is now widely practiced in the new-age community. Beyond physical postures (asanas), yoga incorporates breath control (pranayama), meditation, and ethical guidelines (yamas and niyamas) to achieve spiritual enlightenment. The resurgence of ancient practices in modern contexts is really notable nowadays. Shamanism, which is one of the oldest spiritual practices, has also experienced a revival. Modern shamans conduct ceremonies and rituals, such as drum circles and plant medicine ceremonies, to facilitate healing and spiritual awakening. These practices often involve altered states of consciousness and the belief in spirit guides and animal totems.

But if altered states sound too far out for you, there is also reiki, which is a modern spiritual practice that was developed in Japan. It involves channeling universal life energy through the hands to promote healing and balance. Practitioners believe that this energy can alleviate physical, emotional, and spiritual imbalances.

Of course, modern spiritual practices also reflect the integration of technology and contemporary lifestyles with traditional elements. Digital spirituality has emerged, with online meditation sessions, virtual reality spiritual experiences, and apps designed for mindfulness and spiritual growth. These platforms provide accessibility and convenience that allow you to engage in spiritual practices from the comfort of your home.

Ecospirituality is also a modern practice that combines environmentalism with spirituality. It emphasizes the sacredness of the Earth and the interconnectedness of all life forms. Practices include nature meditations, environmental activism, and rituals that honor the Earth, such as solstice celebrations and eco-friendly ceremonies. It's like a marriage between several spiritual practices, which is more commonly known as interfaith spirituality. This represents another modern trend where individuals draw from multiple religious and spiritual traditions to create a personalized spiritual path. This eclectic approach allows for a diverse and inclusive spirituality that respects and integrates different beliefs and practices. It is becoming exceedingly popular as people come to the conclusion that all faiths and practices have merit.

Practical Steps for Exploring Spiritual Paths

Exploring different spiritual paths involves a combination of research, personal reflection, and experiential learning. There are various avenues you can take to discover and deepen your understanding of different spiritual traditions, practices, and teachings. Just know that the journey is highly personal and can be enriched by utilizing diverse resources. Visiting sacred sites and engaging with communities are also great options here.

When it comes to reading and research, there is a wealth of literature available on various spiritual traditions, including books, articles, and online resources. Libraries, bookstores, and online platforms such as Amazon or Google Books offer an extensive range of materials. I would recommend that you seek out foundational texts of different religions and spiritual movements, such as the Bible, Quran, Bhagavad Gita, Tao Te Ching, and works by contemporary spiritual authors like Deepak Chopra, Eckhart Tolle, and Thich Nhat Hanh. Additionally, academic texts and historical accounts can provide context and a deeper understanding of these traditions.

Another valuable resource is the internet, of course. You can find websites, forums, and online courses dedicated to exploring spirituality. Websites like Patheos, Beliefnet, and

Spirituality & Health offer articles and discussions on a wide variety of spiritual topics. Online platforms like Coursera and edX provide courses on world religions, mindfulness, meditation, and other spiritual practices. These courses often include lectures, readings, and interactive elements that can help deepen your understanding.

Remember that visiting places of worship and sacred sites is a great way to really immerse yourself in the practice. Many cities have temples, churches, mosques, synagogues, and other places of worship that welcome visitors. Attending services, ceremonies, or community events can give you firsthand experience of different practices and beliefs. Additionally, sacred sites around the world, such as Stonehenge, Machu Picchu, Varanasi, Mecca, and Jerusalem, offer unique opportunities for spiritual exploration and connection. Just be mindful of the places that you are going to. Do your research and, if possible, go with a guide so that you don't run the risk of committing what the respective peoples would consider spiritually impure acts on their holy lands. This is a great opportunity to engage with spiritual communities. Joining a local meditation group, yoga class, or spiritual discussion group can provide support and companionship on your journey. These communities often offer workshops and retreats that can deepen your understanding and practice.

If not a guide, try to find a spiritual mentor for guidance. Many traditions have experienced practitioners or teachers who can answer questions and provide personalized instruction. Seek out teachers who resonate with you, whether they are local leaders, authors, or online instructors. Attending workshops, retreats, and seminars led by these teachers can provide immersive experiences and deepen your understanding. But experimentation and personal practice are crucial for discovering what resonates with you. Try different meditation techniques, mindfulness practices, prayer, chanting, or ritual ceremonies. Reflect on how these practices make you feel and what insights they bring. Journaling your experiences can help track your progress and identify patterns or preferences.

To determine if a certain spiritual teaching is right for you, pay attention to your intuition and inner experiences. Notice how the teachings resonate with you emotionally, intellectually, and spiritually. Do they bring you peace and a sense of connection? Do they align with your values and life experiences? Trusting your inner guidance is key to finding a path that truly nourishes your soul.

In essence, exploring different spiritual paths is a deeply personal experience. By utilizing a variety of resources, engaging with communities, seeking guidance, and experimenting with different practices, you can discover what suits you and create a spiritual path that is uniquely your own.

Finding What Resonates with You

Using the idea of values and beliefs that we addressed in the early sections of the book, you can find what resonates with you by engaging in a process of introspection, exploration, and experimentation. This journey involves understanding your core values, examining your belief systems, and then aligning your actions and choices with these insights to create a life that is authentically yours.

So, go back and reflect on your core values again. Remember, values are the fundamental principles that guide your behavior and decision-making. They are deeply rooted in your experiences, upbringing, and intrinsic motivations. To identify your values, think back to moments when you felt truly happy or fulfilled. What were you doing? Who were you with? What aspects of those moments stand out to you? For example, if you felt proud when helping someone in need, compassion might be one of your core values. If you've ever felt fulfilled when creating something new, creativity might be another key value for you.

Next, examine your belief systems. Remember that beliefs are the convictions or acceptance that certain things are true or real, often without immediate evidence. These can be religious, philosophical, or personal beliefs about how the world works and your place in it. Consider the beliefs you currently hold and question their origins. Are they inherited from your family, shaped by your culture, or developed through your personal experiences? Reflect on whether these beliefs still serve you or if they need re-evaluation. For instance, you might have been taught to believe in a strict work ethic, but through reflection, you might realize the importance of balance and self-care in your life.

Once you have a clearer understanding of your values and beliefs, the next step is to explore different avenues to see what resonates with you. This might involve engaging with various philosophies, spiritual practices, or lifestyles to find what aligns with your internal compass. For example, if you value inner peace and have a belief in the interconnectedness of all things, exploring mindfulness practices or meditation might resonate with you.

Attend workshops, read books, join discussion groups, and expose yourself to different perspectives to broaden your understanding.

I'll reiterate that experimentation is key in finding what resonates with you. Try out different activities, practices, or ways of thinking to see how they make you feel. Pay attention to your emotional responses, mental clarity, and overall well-being. If practicing yoga brings you a sense of calm and connection, it might be an indication that it aligns with your values and beliefs. If volunteering makes you feel fulfilled and purposeful, it's a sign that service to others is an important aspect of your life.

As you explore and experiment, it's essential to stay attuned to your intuition. Your intuition is your inner guide and it helps you discern what feels right for you. Trust your gut feelings and instincts when making decisions about what to pursue and what to let go of. If something feels off or doesn't bring you joy, it's okay to move on and try something else. Your journey is unique, and there is no one-size-fits-all approach. As you grow and evolve, your values and beliefs might shift, and that's perfectly natural. Regularly check in with yourself to ensure that you are living in alignment with your true self. Journaling, meditating, or having deep conversations with trusted friends can help you stay connected to your core.

Finding what resonates with you also involves setting boundaries and making choices that honor your values and beliefs. This can be challenging, especially when faced with external pressures from family, society, or work. However, staying true to yourself is essential for your personal fulfillment.

*

Now that you have begun to tap into the spiritual paths available to you, we can move on to the final section of our book. As you prepare yourself for the road ahead, always remember that your quest for meaning is a personal one. No matter how you choose to manifest your spiritual self, that is for you to judge. After all, only you know what experiences you have lived through and what brings you toward your most energetically aligned self.

Part IV: The Road Ahead

CHAPTER 10 –
CREATIVITY IS SPIRITUALITY

People often ask whether anything other than religion can be regarded as a spiritual pursuit and my answer to that is a resounding "Yes!" Spirituality is made up of the things that make your soul feel most alive and at ease — where you are not in competition with anyone and the only person that you want to be better than is the person you were yesterday. Spirituality is about tapping into that higher realm of existence and creative pursuits are a sure-fire way to do this.

Whether it is writing poetry, lip-syncing, dancing, singing, painting, sketching, landscaping — whatever it is that makes you feel alive, do it! Creativity is unique to humankind. In fact, some say that creativity is what sets us apart from all other living beings in existence. That is because we don't create like the weaver bird who creates beautiful nests for a mate or the penguin who seeks out a perfect pebble for a mate. We create for the joy of creating and that is true whether someone gets to see that creation or not.

Connection Between Creativity & Spirituality

Spirituality and creativity are intertwined and each one feeds and enriches the other. The connection between the two can be seen in the lives of many renowned artists, dancers, and composers who have demonstrated a deep spiritual nature and a heightened sense of calm in their creative processes. When you think about it, it's easy to see how the two elements are linked. Spirituality, at its core, involves a search for meaning, purpose, and connection beyond the material world. It is about finding a deeper sense of self and a relationship with the universe, the divine, or whatever one perceives as greater than oneself. Creativity, on the other hand, is the expression of this deeper self. It is the act of bringing something new into existence, whether through art, music, dance, writing, or other forms of artistic endeavor. When spirituality and creativity merge, they create a powerful synergy that can lead to transformative works of art.

Consider the example of Vincent van Gogh. He was a painter whose works were infused with a deep sense of spirituality and emotional intensity. Van Gogh often spoke of his desire to capture the divine in his paintings. His famous work "Starry Night" is a testament to his attempt to depict the vast, swirling cosmos and the beauty he perceived in the natural world. Van Gogh's spirituality was not tied to traditional religious practices, but rather to his own personal sense of the sacred in everyday life. His creative process was a form of meditation that allowed him to connect with his inner self despite his turbulent mental state.

Similarly, the composer Ludwig van Beethoven found solace and spiritual fulfillment in his music. Despite his deafness, which isolated him from the world, Beethoven's compositions are marked by their emotional depth and spiritual grandeur. His Ninth Symphony, with its "Ode to Joy," is an ode to the transcendent power of human connection and the divine. Beethoven's ability to create such moving and powerful music in the face of personal adversity speaks to his deep resilience and connection to his creative muse.

There is also Martha Graham, who revolutionized the art of dance with her innovative techniques and expressive choreography. Graham's work was deeply influenced by her spiritual beliefs and her exploration of human emotions. She viewed dance as a spiritual act and a way to communicate deep truths about the human experience. Her choreography often delved into themes of myth, psychology, and the human condition — creating a bridge between the physical and the spiritual.

The poet Rainer Maria Rilke was much the same way. Rilke's writings are filled with spiritual imagery and introspective exploration. He believed that true creativity came from a deep inner necessity that he termed a "spiritual calling" to express the inexpressible. Rilke's letters and poems often explored the idea of the artist as a conduit for the divine, thus, capturing fleeting moments of transcendence and insight.

These examples illustrate how spirituality can serve as a wellspring of creativity that provides artists with a deeper sense of purpose and connection. Spirituality encourages introspection and mindfulness, which can help artists tap into their subconscious and access a richer, more nuanced creative expression. By engaging in spiritual practices such as meditation, prayer, or spending time in nature, artists can quiet their minds, open their hearts, and connect with their inner selves and the universe. This state of calm and centeredness can lead to moments of inspiration and clarity, where creativity flows naturally and effortlessly. The connection between spirituality and creativity also has practical benefits for artists. Engaging in spiritual practices can help reduce stress, enhance mental clarity, and encourage emotional resilience. By cultivating a sense of inner peace and well-being, artists can navigate the challenges and uncertainties of the creative process with greater ease and confidence. This, in turn, can lead to more authentic and meaningful artistic expression.

Engaging in Artistic Pursuits

As you now know, engaging in artistic pursuits can serve as a form of spiritual practice because they open your mind and heart to new dimensions of awareness and growth. For those who may be skeptical or resistant to traditional forms of spirituality, art can act as a bridge that connects you to deeper aspects of yourself and the universe. Whether through painting, music, dance, writing, or any other form of creative expression, artistic pursuits can facilitate a journey toward becoming the spiritual person you aspire to be.

Art, in its many forms, is a powerful tool for self-expression and exploration. When you engage in artistic activities, you tap into your inner world — accessing emotions, thoughts, and sensations that might otherwise remain hidden. This process of exploration is inherently spiritual because it involves delving into the depths of your being and uncovering truths about yourself and your place in the world. Artistic expression allows you to confront and process complex feelings, which can lead to greater self-awareness and emotional healing.

One of the most significant ways in which artistic pursuits can serve as a spiritual practice is by allowing for a state of mindfulness and presence. When you are deeply engrossed in creating art, you enter a state of flow where time seems to stand still and your mind is fully focused on the present moment. This state of flow is similar to the meditative state achieved through traditional spiritual practices. By regularly engaging in artistic activities, you can cultivate a sense of mindfulness that extends beyond the creative process and into your daily life. Moreover, artistic pursuits can open your mind to new perspectives and ways of thinking. As you experiment with different forms of art, you learn to see the world in new and varied ways. This expanded perception can help you break free from rigid thought patterns and embrace a more open, flexible, and creative mindset. I firmly believe that this openness is a crucial component of spiritual growth because it allows you to be receptive to new ideas, experiences, and insights that can deepen your understanding of yourself and the world around you.

When all is said and done, art serves as a bridge between your current self and the spiritual person you hope to become by providing a means of exploring and expressing your spiritual beliefs and aspirations. Through artistic expression, you can visualize and articulate your spiritual journey, thus, creating a tangible representation of your inner transformation. This process of externalizing your spiritual experiences can make them feel more real and accessible, which can help you to integrate them into your everyday life. In fact, some people consider the actual act of creating art a form of devotion or prayer because it is their way of connecting with the divine or the sacred. Many artists describe their creative process as a spiritual experience, where they feel guided by a higher power or a sense of something greater than themselves. By approaching art with a sense of reverence and intention, you can transform your creative practice into a spiritual ritual that nourishes your soul and strengthens your connection to the divine. The more you tap into this side of yourself, the more adept you'll become at connecting to your higher power through creative pursuits. And the truth is that it doesn't matter what or whom your higher power is. You don't even have to know their name to know that you are being guided by them. Remember, trust your intuition!

In essence, engaging in artistic pursuits can be a transformative spiritual practice that opens your mind and heart to new possibilities. You just have to be willing to experience it.

Using Creativity to Express Yourself

Using creativity to express yourself is a powerful tool, especially when you are still learning how to manage your emotions on your spiritual journey. Creativity can serve as a therapeutic outlet, a form of self-discovery, and a way to process and understand your emotional experiences. Engaging in creative activities can help you navigate your inner landscape by offering clarity and relief as you grow spiritually and emotionally.

When you are on a spiritual journey, managing your emotions can often feel overwhelming. Emotions can be complex and difficult to articulate, but creative expression allows you to convey what words sometimes cannot. Through art, music, writing, dance, and other forms of creativity, you can give shape and form to your feelings. This can make them more tangible and easier to understand. This process can be incredibly cathartic — helping you release pent-up emotions and gain insights into your inner world.

One of the first steps in using creativity to express yourself is to choose a medium that resonates with you. This could be anything from painting and drawing to playing an instrument, writing poetry, or dancing. The key is to find a form of creative expression that feels natural and enjoyable for you. Once you have chosen your medium, allow yourself to explore it without judgment or expectations. Creativity is about the process, not the outcome, so give yourself permission to experiment and play.

Journaling is a particularly effective creative practice for emotional expression and it serves as an easy gateway to creativity if you don't consider yourself particularly creative in nature. Keeping a journal allows you to write freely about your thoughts and feelings, providing a safe space to explore your emotions. You can use your journal to reflect on your spiritual journey, document your experiences, and express your inner struggles and triumphs. Over time, journaling can help you gain a deeper understanding of your emotional patterns and triggers, thus, offering valuable insights that can guide your spiritual growth.

Visual art, such as painting or drawing, is another powerful way to express your emotions creatively. When you create visual art, you can use colors, shapes, and textures to represent your feelings. For example, bright, bold colors might reflect joy and excitement, while darker, muted tones could convey sadness or introspection. The act of putting brush to canvas or pencil to paper can be meditative — allowing you to enter a state of flow where you are fully immersed in the present moment. This state of flow can be deeply healing, thus, helping you process and release emotions.

Music and dance are also excellent forms of creative expression for managing emotions. Playing an instrument, singing, or dancing allows you to connect with your body and express your emotions physically. Music can evoke powerful emotions and provide a soundtrack for your spiritual journey, while dance can help you release tension and stress. Both music and dance can be incredibly freeing because they allow you to express yourself in ways that words cannot.

Collage and mixed media art can also be powerful tools for emotional expression. Creating a collage from magazines, photographs, and found objects allows you to visually represent your emotions and experiences. You can create a vision board that reflects your spiritual goals and aspirations, or a mood board that captures your current emotional state. Mixed media art encourages you to think outside the box and use a variety of materials, thus, offering a rich and dynamic way to express yourself. The different fonts, color schemes, and imagery can help you release an array of pent-up emotions. You might also find that the process of ripping through magazine pages, as opposed to cutting them, adds an extra edge to this.

Whatever you choose, engaging in creative activities regularly can help you build emotional resilience and develop healthier coping mechanisms. Creativity encourages you to confront and process your emotions, rather than suppressing or ignoring them. By expressing your feelings through art, you can gain a deeper awareness of yourself and your spiritual journey.

Incorporating creativity into your spiritual practice can also help you connect with your intuition and inner wisdom. When you create, you tap into a deeper part of yourself, thus, accessing insights and guidance that might not be available through rational thought alone. This intuitive connection can provide valuable direction. Use it wisely.

*

With a broader understanding of the link between our creative nature and our spiritual nature, you'll find that many of the acts that you have committed in your life were (in essence) spiritual. You see, as I said at the very beginning of this book, you have meaning and purpose simply because you exist. The further down this rabbit hole you go, the more you will see that it is not some grand gesture that makes your life meaningful, but the richness with which you experience the little things.

CHAPTER 11 –
ACTS OF KINDNESS & SERVICE

From looking within — with your sense of self and creativity — we move on to looking outside of yourself. When it comes to finding meaning, there are ways in which we can find meaning outside of ourselves. But there is a catch to it. You are not actually looking for the meaning outside of yourself but you are looking for the meaning in the actions you take with others (which, in essence, is outside of yourself).

I'm talking about acts of kindness and service.

Human beings, like several other species, enjoy caring for and protecting others. We found incredible amounts of joy in the acts of service that we commit and our ability to bring a smile to the faces of others. Being of service to people can provide your life with an added sense of meaning. Well, in actuality, it simply reminds you of the meaning that your life already has. It shows you that you are needed even when you think you aren't and helps spiritually aligned.

Spiritual Benefits of Kindness & Altruism

Kindness and altruism are important aspects of a fulfilling and spiritually enriched life. The spiritual benefits of these virtues extend beyond the immediate impact on others — influencing your own spiritual growth. Engaging in acts of kindness and altruism creates a deep sense of connection with others. When you perform kind acts, you create a ripple effect of positivity and compassion, thus, enhancing the interconnectedness of your community. This sense of connection is crucial for spiritual development because it reinforces the understanding that all beings are part of a larger whole. Recognizing and honoring this interconnectedness can lead to a greater sense of unity and oneness, which is a core principle in many spiritual traditions.

Practicing kindness and altruism also cultivates inner peace and happiness. When you help others without expecting anything in return, you experience a sense of fulfillment and joy. This selfless giving aligns with the principle of non-attachment, which is a key tenet in many spiritual philosophies. By letting go of the expectation of reciprocation, you free yourself from the cycle of desire and disappointment. This allows a state of contentment and tranquility to emerge. This inner peace is a foundational aspect of spiritual well-being because it enables you to navigate obstacles with grace and resilience.

Furthermore, kindness and altruism promote the development of empathy and compassion. Empathy involves understanding and sharing the feelings of others, while compassion goes a step further — prompting you to take action to alleviate their suffering. These qualities are essential for spiritual growth as they encourage you to move beyond self-centered concerns and focus on the well-being of others. Through empathy and compassion, you develop a loving and open heart, which is central to many spiritual practices.

Kindness and altruism also have the power to transform your perspective on life. When you engage in selfless acts, you shift your focus from what you can gain to what you can give. This shift in perspective can lead to a greater appreciation for the simple joys in life and a deeper sense of gratitude. Gratitude, in turn, enhances your spiritual practice by encouraging a positive mindset and opening your heart to the abundance of blessings in your life. It can actually be considered a form of spiritual discipline. Just as meditation and prayer require consistent effort and dedication, so too does the practice of kindness. By making a conscious effort to be kind and selfless, you develop qualities such as patience, humility, and forgiveness. These virtues are essential for spiritual maturity and help you to become a more compassionate and loving person.

With time, these acts can serve as a form of spiritual purification. Many spiritual traditions emphasize the importance of purifying the mind and heart from negative tendencies such as anger, jealousy, and greed. By engaging in kind and selfless actions, you counteract these negative tendencies and cultivate positive qualities such as love, generosity, and compassion. This process of purification helps to cleanse your spirit and elevate your consciousness. However, on a deeper level, kindness and altruism can lead to a sense of purpose and meaning in life. When you dedicate yourself to the service of others, you align your actions with a higher purpose. This sense of purpose can be deeply fulfilling and will provide a strong foundation for spiritual growth. Knowing that your actions are making a positive difference in the lives of others can inspire you to continue on your spiritual path with renewed vigor and commitment.

Identifying Opportunities to Serve Others

Identifying opportunities to serve others is a meaningful way to enhance personal growth, encourage community connections, and cultivate a spirit of kindness and altruism. One of the first steps in identifying opportunities to serve others is to develop a mindset of awareness and attentiveness. By being present in the moment and observing your surroundings, you can become more attuned to the needs of those around you. This heightened awareness allows you to notice when someone might need assistance — whether it's a colleague struggling with a heavy workload, a neighbor who could use help with their groceries, or a friend going through a tough time. Developing this habit of mindfulness helps you recognize moments where your support can make a significant difference.

Listening actively is another crucial aspect of finding ways to serve. Often, people may not explicitly ask for help, but their words, tone, and body language can convey their needs. By practicing active listening, you can pick up on these cues and offer your assistance accordingly. Engage in conversations with genuine interest, ask open-ended questions, and show empathy and understanding. This approach not only helps you identify opportunities to serve but also strengthens your relationships and builds trust.

Volunteering is a structured way to serve others and can be a fulfilling and impactful experience. Look for local organizations, charities, or community groups that align with your interests and values. Whether it's volunteering at a food bank, mentoring youth, participating in environmental clean-up efforts, or offering your skills for free, there are countless ways to get involved. Websites like VolunteerMatch, Idealist, and local community boards can provide a wealth of information about available volunteer opportunities. By dedicating your time and energy to these causes, you can make a positive impact and discover new ways to serve. Networking and building connections with like-minded individuals in this manner can also lead to opportunities to serve. Attend community events, join clubs or organizations related to your interests, and participate in social or professional groups. Engaging with a network of people who share your values can expose you to various service opportunities and inspire collaborative efforts to address common goals. By connecting with others who are passionate about making a difference, you can amplify your impact and find new ways to contribute.

Try to leverage your unique skills and talents to serve others. Consider what you are good at and how those abilities can benefit others. If you have expertise in a particular field, offer free workshops or mentoring sessions. If you are creative, consider organizing community art projects or performances. If you have technical skills, help others with tasks such as website design or computer troubleshooting. By using your talents to serve, you can provide valuable assistance and make a meaningful contribution.

You can also reflect on your passions and values to guide your service efforts. Think about the causes that matter most to you and the issues you feel passionate about. Whether it's social justice, education, healthcare, or environmental sustainability, aligning your service with your passions ensures that your efforts are driven by genuine motivation and commitment. This alignment not only makes your service more impactful but also deeply fulfilling.

However, sometimes, serving others can be as simple as being proactive in your daily life. Small acts of kindness, such as holding the door open for someone, offering a seat on public transportation, or lending a hand to a stranger in need, can create a ripple effect of goodwill. These seemingly minor gestures can brighten someone's day and contribute to a culture of kindness and support within your community. This brings me to my next point.

Integrating Acts of Service into Your Daily Life

Integrating acts of service into daily life is a powerful way to deepen your sense of purpose, connection, and fulfillment. Firstly, start with small acts of kindness. These can be as simple as those small gestures I just mentioned. As stated, they will not only brighten someone else's day but also create a habit of looking for opportunities to assist others in everyday situations.

One innovative approach is to leave positive notes in public places. Carry a small notebook or a stack of sticky notes with you and whenever you have a spare moment, write a few kind words or an inspiring message. Then, discreetly place these notes in locations where others will find them, such as inside library books, on bathroom mirrors, or on park benches. This small gesture can brighten someone's day and create a ripple effect of positivity. Imagine a person finding an unexpected note that says, "You are enough just as you are," or "Believe in your dreams." These simple messages can have a huge positive impact on those who find them. They can provide a moment of encouragement and joy in someone's daily life.

You can also consider incorporating kindness into your daily commute. Whether you drive, bike, or take public transportation, there are numerous opportunities to practice kindness. For drivers, this might mean letting someone merge ahead of you in heavy traffic or paying for the toll of the car behind you. If you use public transport, offering your seat to someone who needs it more or striking up a friendly conversation with a fellow passenger can be wonderful acts of kindness. Bikers can slow down and offer assistance to someone who looks lost or help out with directions. These small, considerate actions can significantly ease the stress of commuting and make everyone's day a little brighter.

So, as you can see, incorporating acts of kindness into your daily life doesn't have to be grandiose or time-consuming. By leaving positive notes in public places, sharing your unique skills with others, and practicing kindness during your commute, you can make a significant impact on the world around you. These novel approaches not only bring joy to others but also enhance your own sense of purpose and fulfillment. Engaging in these creative acts of kindness helps to build a more connected, compassionate, and supportive community.

Lastly, practice self-reflection and gratitude. Take time each day to reflect on the opportunities you've had to serve others and the impact it has had, no matter how small. Cultivate gratitude for the ability to make a positive difference in someone's life and let this gratitude fuel your ongoing commitment to service. As you continue integrating acts of service into your daily life, you not only contribute to the well-being of others but also enhance your own sense of purpose and fulfillment. Each small act of kindness and generosity has the potential to create a ripple effect of positivity, thus, encouraging a more compassionate and supportive community for everyone.

*

At the end of the day, human beings want to live a life of service. We want to help as many people as we can. While charity begins at home, it's important to share the light that you have with the world. As we light the wicks of other candles, we provide ourselves with more light and more warmth. This is without a doubt the first step towards bringing spirituality into your everyday life.

CHAPTER 12 –

BRINGING SPIRITUALITY INTO EVERYDAY LIFE

It's all well and good to have special times of the day or special days that are reserved for meditation and acts of service, but now you need to think about how you can bring spirituality into your everyday life. How do you incorporate these ways of being into your daily routines and daily interactions with others?

At first, it may seem fairly straightforward. However with time, you'll find yourself experiencing moments of irritability, frustration, and even anger that lead you astray from the enlightened side of yourself that you're hoping to be. Many people find it hard to remain so "enlightened" on a daily basis, so I have a secret solution to this problem.

The solution is that you simply don't.

Don't try to be enlightened at every turn. Don't judge yourself for having normal human emotions. Spiritual people understand that everything is a part of the process of being human. They do not need to remain within one emotional wavelength throughout their lives because they understand that monotony is madness.

And so, let's find ways to incorporate spirituality into everyday life without trying to hold yourself to impossible standards.

Practical Ways to Incorporate Spirituality

Incorporating spirituality into your everyday routines is about creating a mindful approach to daily activities and infusing moments with intention and reflection. There are a few steps that you can take to accomplish this but, as always, remember that you should do what feels right to you.

1. **Morning Rituals**: Begin your day with a spiritual practice that sets a positive tone. This could include meditation, prayer, or simply taking a few moments to reflect on your intentions for the day ahead. Starting your morning with mindfulness helps center your mind and spirit before diving into daily tasks.

2. **Gratitude Practice**: Incorporate gratitude into your daily routine by keeping a gratitude journal or taking a few minutes each day to mentally list things that you're thankful for. Acknowledging and appreciating the blessings in your life creates a sense of spiritual connection and contentment.

3. **Nature Connection**: Spend time outdoors and connect with nature as a spiritual practice. Whether it's a walk in the park, gardening, or simply sitting in a quiet spot surrounded by greenery, immersing yourself in nature can be deeply grounding and rejuvenating.

4. **Evening Reflection**: Conclude your day with a moment of reflection or prayer to review the events of the day and express gratitude for both challenges and blessings. This practice promotes introspection, emotional processing, and a sense of closure before bedtime.

5. **Sacred Space**: Create a sacred space in your home — a quiet corner, an altar, or a designated room where you can retreat for moments of prayer, meditation, or spiritual contemplation. Designing this space with meaningful objects and symbols enhances its spiritual significance.

Of course, there are more ways that you can incorporate spirituality into daily life, many of which we've explored all throughout this book. You might even have a few ideas of your own brewing and this is a good sign that you're beginning to tap into thoughts that align with your sense of spirituality. By incorporating these practical ways to infuse spirituality into your everyday routines, you will find that you begin to experience a deeper sense of connection, purpose, and inner peace. These small but consistent practices not only nurture your spiritual side but also enrich your overall quality of life. They will help you navigate daily challenges with grace and mindfulness.

From here, you can begin creating spiritual rituals and habits that speak to you.

Creating Spiritual Rituals & Habits

Creating spiritual rituals and habits is a way to enrich your spiritual life and enhance your overall well-being. It begins with setting clear intentions, which act as a guide for your practices. These intentions align your actions with your values and spiritual aspirations, whatever they may be. Before you consider creating these rituals, I would like you to keep in mind that consistency plays a crucial role in integrating spiritual rituals into daily life. Establishing a routine ensures that these practices become a natural part of your day, but they must be just that: routine. Whether you engage in morning meditation, evening prayer, or weekly reflections, keep at it and try to maintain the ritual even if you're experiencing challenging moments. Routine provides structure and discipline, which reinforces the importance of your spiritual journey in your everyday experience.

Creating a sacred space within your home or environment is one of those essential elements for uninterrupted spiritual practice. As mentioned, this space can be simple. You can choose to designate a corner with a cushion for meditation, an altar adorned with meaningful objects for deep thought, or a serene outdoor spot that connects you with nature and the universe. The goal is to signal your brain that it's time to switch gears. Sometimes, these designated areas act as visual cues that help us transition from being the myriads of other things that we have to be throughout the day to just spiritual beings.

Either way, try to approach your spiritual rituals with mindful presence and awareness. Being fully present in the moment enhances the significance of your actions, whether you're chanting, lighting candles, or practicing yoga. Mindfulness deepens your spiritual experience, thus, allowing you to immerse yourself fully in the practice at hand. Infuse your rituals with symbolism that resonates with your beliefs and values. Symbols such as sacred objects, elements of nature, or meaningful gestures can evoke a sense of reverence and connection. Just be aware that personalization is key to ensuring that your rituals and habits are meaningful and relevant to your spiritual path. Tailor your practices to suit your preferences and evolving needs over time. Experiment with and adapt them as necessary. This will allow your spiritual practices to grow organically with your journey.

After engaging in your spiritual rituals, take time to reflect on your experiences and insights. Journaling, contemplation, or discussing with a trusted friend supports deeper understanding and integration of the spiritual lessons learned. Reflection enhances self-awareness and encourages continued growth on your spiritual path. Seek community and support from like-minded individuals or spiritual groups. Participating in group rituals, discussions, or retreats will provide opportunities for communal support, shared wisdom, and collective spiritual growth. Connecting with others who share your beliefs enriches your spiritual practices and inspires ongoing exploration.

Just try to remain adaptable and flexible in your spiritual journey. Embrace new practices, integrate diverse perspectives, and evolve your rituals as you gain new insights and experiences. Spiritual growth requires openness to change and exploration to deepen your connection with spirituality.

The Ugly Side of the Ongoing Spiritual Journey

As you prepare to wrap up this guide, there is something you should remember. Going on a spiritual journey isn't always a serene and uplifting experience. It can also be fraught with challenges, doubts, and moments of frustration. This journey often entails confronting uncomfortable truths about yourself and the world as well as navigating inner turmoil and dealing with the imperfections of human nature as a whole.

One of the most poignant struggles on the spiritual path is the oscillation between personal growth and the realization that others may not share the same quest for meaning. This can lead to feelings of isolation, disappointment, or even anger towards those who seem indifferent or resistant to introspection and growth. Witnessing apathy or superficiality in others' lives can evoke a sense of frustration as you yearn for deeper connections and meaningful interactions that align with your spiritual aspirations.

Moreover, the process of self-discovery often involves confronting shadow aspects of yourself — unresolved emotions, past traumas, or negative patterns of behavior. Delving into these depths can be unsettling and emotionally taxing — stirring up feelings of fear, sadness, or discomfort. Confronting your vulnerabilities and flaws requires courage and resilience. Don't forget how difficult that can be. As this path challenges long-held beliefs and invites introspection, you will feel out of sorts.

The pursuit of spiritual growth may also unearth existential questions and uncertainties about life's purpose and the nature of reality. Wrestling with existential dilemmas, such as mortality, suffering, or the existence of higher powers, can provoke existential angst or existential crisis. These moments of existential questioning may evoke feelings of anxiety, confusion, or even despair as you grapple with the mysteries of the universe. To make matters worse, the spiritual journey often involves letting go of attachments and expectations that no longer serve your growth. This process of detachment can be painful because it may require releasing relationships, habits, or beliefs that once provided comfort but now hinder spiritual progress. Grieving the loss of familiar comforts and facing the unknown future can make you feel deeply sad. It might even prompt you to resist all of the wonderful changes that you have begun implementing in your life.

Yes, navigating the complexities of spiritual teachings and practices can also lead to that level of confusion or disillusionment. The diversity of spiritual paths and teachings may create ambiguity or inner conflict as you discern which beliefs and practices resonate most deeply with your authentic self. This exploration requires critical reflection that is, quite frankly, emotionally draining and taxing. As you navigate the nuances and contradictions inherent in spiritual teachings, the pursuit of spiritual enlightenment or higher consciousness can sometimes create a sense of spiritual bypassing or escapism. But avoiding uncomfortable emotions or worldly responsibilities in favor of spiritual pursuits may lead to a disconnection from lived experiences and genuine emotional processing that is on offer to us out in the world. This imbalance can hinder holistic growth and perpetuate a cycle of avoidance rather than authentic transformation.

However, despite all of these challenges, acknowledging the "ugly side" of the spiritual journey is essential for genuine growth and resilience. Embracing the complexities, uncertainties, and discomforts of the journey will drive humility and empathy. Plus, you'll have a deeper sense of self-awareness. That inner strength and fortitude will empower you to go through the pitfalls of adversity with grace and compassion. It truly is a catalyst for your growth and spiritual evolution. By confronting inner shadows, grappling with existential questions, and navigating interpersonal dynamics, you develop resilience, authenticity, and a deeper understanding of both yourself and the world around you.

*

And that is all that you need to know for now. If you feel the need to take your quest for meaning further than this, I wholeheartedly encourage you to do so. However, if you're feeling overwhelmed by just what is in these pages alone, start at Chapter 1 again and take your time with each subsequent chapter. There is no expiration date for growth. Go at your own pace.

IN CLOSING

As we reach the end of the road together, it's essential to reflect on the key insights we've uncovered. Throughout this book, we have gone deep into the nature of spirituality and its role in our quest for meaning beyond the material world. We've explored diverse spiritual paths, examined our values and beliefs, and learned how to integrate spirituality into our daily lives. The essence of our journey — as we've uncovered — is to recognize that spirituality is an evolving pursuit that guides us toward a more meaningful and fulfilling life.

What you should know now is that the journey does not end here. Spirituality is not a destination but a continuous process of self-discovery and growth. Embrace the practice of regular reflection. Ask yourself: *What new insights have I gained? How have my values and beliefs evolved? What practices resonate with me most?* By maintaining a habit of introspection, you allow yourself to adapt and grow, thus, remaining open to new experiences and understandings. Remember, your spiritual path is unique to you and there is always room for development and transformation.

Living authentically means aligning your actions with your true values and beliefs. It involves being honest with yourself and others, embracing your uniqueness, and letting go of societal expectations that do not serve you. When you live authentically, you create a life that is rich in meaning and fulfillment. Coupled with a sense of purpose, this authenticity can guide you through the highs and lows with a deep sense of inner peace and contentment.

As you continue on your spiritual journey, remember that you are not alone. Every step you take towards understanding yourself and the world around you contributes to a greater collective consciousness. Stay curious, keep learning, and be kind to yourself along the way. Challenges may arise, but they are opportunities for growth and deeper understanding. Trust in your path, have faith in your inner wisdom, and remain open to the beauty and wonder of life.

May you find the courage to live your truth, the wisdom to seek meaning, and the compassion to connect deeply with yourself and others. Your journey is a testament to your commitment to living a purposeful and spiritually enriched life. Continue forward with confidence, knowing that the quest for meaning is a lifelong adventure filled with endless possibilities

APPENDIX: ADDITIONAL RESOURCES

Books

1. **The Power of Now** by Eckhart Tolle

2. **The Four Agreements** by Don Miguel Ruiz

3. **The Untethered Soul** by Michael A. Singer

4. **Man's Search for Meaning** by Viktor E. Frankl

5. **The Art of Happiness** by Dalai Lama and Howard Cutler

6. **A New Earth: Awakening to Your Life's Purpose** by Eckhart Tolle

7. **The Book of Joy** by Dalai Lama and Desmond Tutu

8. **The Tao of Pooh** by Benjamin Hoff

Websites and Online Communities

- o **Mindful.org:** Offers resources on mindfulness meditation, practices, and its benefits for spiritual well-being.

- o **Spirituality & Practice:** A hub for exploring various spiritual traditions and practices, including book reviews, courses, and articles.

- Insight Timer: A meditation app and community offering guided meditations, courses, and talks from spiritual teachers.

- Tiny Buddha: Provides wisdom and insights on mindfulness, personal growth, and finding meaning in everyday life.

- Greater Good Science Center of Berkeley: Explores the science of a meaningful life, offering articles, podcasts, and online courses.

Podcasts and Videos

1. On Being with Krista Tippett

   - A podcast that explores the big questions of meaning, faith, ethics, and what it means to be human.

2. The Tim Ferriss Show

   - Interviews with high achievers discussing their routines, habits, and the search for meaning.

3. SuperSoul Conversations with Oprah

   - Conversations with thought leaders, authors, and spiritual teachers about life's big questions.

4. TED Talks on Spirituality

   - A collection of talks exploring various aspects of spirituality and personal growth.

Courses and Workshops

1. **Coursera: The Science of Well-Being**

   o   A course by Yale University on increasing your own happiness and building more productive habits.

2. **Mindfulness-Based Stress Reduction (MBSR)**

   o   An 8-week course designed to reduce stress and enhance well-being through mindfulness practices.

3. **Sounds True**

   o   Offers online courses and workshops from leading spiritual teachers on various aspects of spirituality.

REFERENCES & CITATIONS

1. Brown, B. (2012). Daring Greatly: How the Courage to Be Vulnerable Transforms the Way We Live, Love, Parent, and Lead. Avery.
2. Gottman, J. M., & Silver, N. (2015). The Seven Principles for Making Marriage Work: A Practical Guide from the Country's Foremost Relationship Expert. Harmony.
3. Neff, K. D. (2011). Self-Compassion: The Proven Power of Being Kind to Yourself. William Morrow.
4. Covey, S. R. (1989). The 7 Habits of Highly Effective People: Powerful Lessons in Personal Change. Simon & Schuster.
5. Van Der Kolk, B. A. (2015). The Body Keeps the Score: Brain, Mind, and Body in the Healing of Trauma. Penguin Books.
6. Lerner, H. (2017). The Dance of Anger: A Woman's Guide to Changing the Patterns of Intimate Relationships. Harper Paperbacks.
7. Johnson, S. M. (2004). The Practice of Emotionally Focused Marital Therapy: Creating Connection. Journal of Clinical Psychology, 60(6), 671–680.
8. Baumeister, R. F., & Leary, M. R. (1995). The Need to Belong: Desire for Interpersonal Attachments as a Fundamental Human Motivation. Psychological Bulletin, 117(3), 497–529.
9. Reis, H. T., & Gable, S. L. (2000). Event-Sampling and Other Methods for Studying Everyday Experience. Handbook of

Research Methods in Social and Personality Psychology, 190–222.

10. Fredrickson, B. L. (2001). The Role of Positive Emotions in Positive Psychology: The Broáden-and-Build Theory of Positive Emotions. American Psychologist, 56(3), 218–226.

11. Collins, N. L., & Feeney, B. C. (2004). Working Models of Attachment Shape Perceptions of Social Support: Evidence from Experimental and Observational Studies. Journal of Personality and Social Psychology, 87(3), 363–383.

Made in United States
North Haven, CT
28 June 2024

54166797R10068